MW01204216

UNCOVERING THE VEIL SERIES

NEPHILIM:

The First Human Clones

Why Their Existence Led to Noah's Flood

MATTHEW OMAYE AJIAKE

SONIKA
PUBLISHING

Sonika Publishing, San Francisco, California

NEPHILIM: The First Human Clones
Published by Sonika Publishing
© 2003 by Matthew Omaye Ajiake

All Scripture quotation in this book, except those noted otherwise, are from the New International Version, © 1973, 1978, 1984 by the International Bible Society. All rights reserved. Used by permission of Zondervan Bible Publishers.

Quotations marked NKJV are from the New King James Version, 1979, 1980, 1982, 1984 by Thomas Nelson, Inc., Publishers.

Quotations marked MSG are Scriptures taken from THE MESSAGE. Copyright notice © 1993, 1994, 1995, 1996. Used by permission of NavPress Publishing Group

Quotations marked (AMP) are taken from The Amplified Bible. Old Testament copyright © 1965, 1987 by the Zondervan Corporation, Grand Rapids, Michigan. New Testament copyright © 1958, 1987 by The Lockman Foundation, La Habra, California.

For information:
SONIKA PUBLISHING
POST OFFICE BOX 7114
FREMONT, CA 94537

WWW.SONIKAPUBLISHING.COM

PRINTED IN HONG KONG

ISBN: 0-9719211-9-9
Library of Congress Control Number: 2003094576

Table of Contents

ACKNOWLEDGEMENTS

A very, very special thank you to my wife and children (Olivia, Jason, Austin, Josiah, and Grace) for their sacrifices during the writing of this book. Special thanks to Jack Lowry of Jack Lowry Designs and Pamela Batliner for your friendship and wisdom throughout the book design process. Thank you Ruhama Vertfort of Logos Editing Service for an editing job well done. Your kindness was contagious. Special thanks to Dick and Sandy Modzeleski of Rainbow Funding and Real Estate Services.

DEDICATION

This book is dedicated to all those in the biomedical and cloning fields as well as to all those who will interact with human clones or advocate for their rights:

My prayer is that you will make a Noah-type difference in your sphere of influence.

INTRODUCTION

We live in one of the most exciting times in history, when ancient stories and biblical prophecies that did not make sense a few short years ago are becoming our reality. One such story and prophetic revelation is about some obscure creatures of Noah's time, the Nephilim.

According to the Bible, the Nephilim came into existence when the sons of God and the daughters of men married and had children who were neither fully the sons of God nor the sons of men. The Nephilim were known for three unique characteristics: "they were giants, heroes of old, and men of renown." The Nephilim were the contemporaries of Noah, and according to the biblical account, bore the main responsibility for God's destruction of the world.

What makes the story of the Nephilim and Noah's world so relevant to us is that over two thousand years after the flood, Jesus, in one of His rare prophetic utterances, declared: "As it was in the days of Noah, so it will be at the coming of the Son of Man."

This means that if, for example, the world before the flood had five-story buildings, we would expect to see five-story buildings, or buildings of a similar height, in our world. This doesn't mean that the buildings would be exactly the same, but that the structure (height) would be the same, as opposed to having the same form (design and architecture). So, if the Nephilim really existed during Noah's day, then we should be able to see the re-emergence of similar unnatural humanoid creatures in our own time.

From the time of the Old Testament up to the late twentieth century, our understanding of the Nephilim story has been that the sons of God who impregnated human women to produced these monsters were fallen angels. So, if Jesus was correct in His prediction, and we believe that we live in the end times, where are these half-angel, half-human creatures in our world today?

While many interpretations of biblical truths that were passed down to us through the ages are non-negotiable, the traditional interpretation of the Nephilim is not one of them. Because it was the end-time world that Jesus compared Noah's world to, the correct interpretation of who the Nephilim were can only be understood in the end time world—our twenty-first century—not in previous generations.

This book discusses various views of the Nephilim. It decodes the Nephilim world, compares it to our twenty-first century world, and offers some strategies—like Noah's—to make a godly difference. Will you join me in an expedition to the past as we uncover the Nephilim world order and discover what form these creatures have taken—or will take in our world?

Chapter 1

DO HALF-GODS, HALF-HUMANS REALLY EXIST?

Have you ever wondered where in the world all the legends and epics about creatures who are half-god, half-human came from? Many scholars of global traditions and history pre-date the origin of these myths to before the time of Noah's flood. Even though some people do not believe that Noah's flood ever really happened, most primitive and modern cultures in the world have stories, legends, myths, and worldviews that originated from this global deluge, which validates its authenticity. Here are some samples:

The Egyptians believed that at one time, the gods purified the earth by means of a great flood, from which only a few shepherds were saved. Fa-He, the founder of Chinese civilization along with his wife, three sons, and three daughters were said to have escaped from a flood, sent because man had revolted against heaven. The people of England tell the legend of the Druids that describes how the world was destroyed by flood because of the wickedness of man, with only a righteous patriarch surviving to repopulate it. The Greeks believed that Deucalion built an ark when he was warned that the gods were going to destroy the earth with a flood. Deucalion survived the flood when his ark rested on Mt. Parnassus. Like Noah, Deucalion also sent a dove out twice to look for dry land.

All these stories raise questions: Why did the gods need to purify the earth? What was the nature of man's revolt against heaven? What wickedness caused the earth to be destroyed? Why did a few humans survive the flood? What did the survivors do right? This is the story of the Nephilim and Noah's world (also called ante diluvian world).

Most of the myths in the world today about half-human, half-something-else creatures originated with the Nephilim story, confirming that mankind does share a common origin. Remember Hercules? Like the other demi-gods—half-man, half-god—of Greek legend, Hercules' tale is rooted in the story of the Nephilim. And just about every culture in the world, folk stories are told about creatures who are half-fish and half-human. They are known as, Mamiwater in Africa, Little Mermaid, probably of Danish origin but popularized in America and the Caribbean, Ningyo in Japan, Asparas in India, Vateo in Polynesia, Lorelei in Germany, halfvine in Norway, and Merrow in Ireland, among others. Even Christopher Columbus wrote about seeing these half-fish, half-human creatures on his voyage to the New World.

While no one today would doubt that dinosaurs once existed or that the Europeans met human beings in the New World (American Indians), no one has ever seen the skeletal remains of half-fish, half-human or angelic-human creatures. Based on the universal distribution of these myths, one would think that these creatures must have actually existed. If they did ever exist, one would expect that their remains would have been found somewhere in the world. If these myths originated from the Nephilim story, the next question becomes: Who were the Nephilim and how can we recognize their existence in our end time world?

Chapter 2

TRADITIONAL VIEWS ABOUT THE NEPHILIM

Genesis 6:4:

The Nephilim were on the earth in those days—and also afterward—when the sons of God went to the daughters of men and had children by them. They were the heroes of old, men of renown. (NIV)

There were giants on the earth in those days, and also afterward, when the sons of God came in to the daughters of men and they bore children to them. Those were the mighty men who were of old, men of renown. (NKJV)

Over the years, the interpretation of this passage about Nephilim has generated its share of controversy among Judeo-Christian scholars. One of the more popular interpretations is that "sons of

God" is a reference to fallen angels who had sexual relationships with human women and thus produced the Nephilim. Then, there are those who believe that the "sons of God" is a reference to the lineage of Seth.

THE FALLEN ANGEL SCHOOL OF THOUGHT

Up to the present time, in light of everything we've known since the time of the Old Testament, the fallen angel school of thought made perfect sense. The fallen angel view draws its greatest support from the Septuagint translators, who converted the original Hebrew Old Testament to the Greek language in 250 B.C., and from the early church fathers. While the fallen angel view is still held by some of the best biblical scholars of our day, in light of our twenty-first century world, it is an impossible view to defend, without applying mythological conclusions to Scriptures as opposed to practical reality.

However, while no one would argue convincingly that demons (fallen angels) do in fact inhabit human bodies, the question remains whether demons could actually change the human genetic makeup of man as God created him. If, for the sake of argument, we accept that the sons of God were fallen angels, what happened to their angelic-human offspring, since only human beings can be restored? Since fallen angels, not being human, were not eligible for either restoration or redemption, Noah's message of righteousness would make no difference to a half-human, half-angelic being. What parts of these creatures' God-imbued spirits and demonic spirits would be eligible for restoration? The fact is that angels and humans are different species. Angels do not have gender; and therefore, they cannot have chromosomes.

Nephilim sighted after the flood

Another evidence used by some who teach that the Nephilim were fallen angels is the testimony of the ten spies who reported to Moses in the wilderness after they spied out the land of Canaan.

Finding the Anakites[1] living there was their proof that either the Nephilim had survived the flood or that the fallen angels had resumed their practice of getting human women pregnant. However, it was only because the Anakites were very tall Arabs that the ten spies compared them to the Nephilim, not because they were actually angel-human hybrids. Furthermore, the ten spies compared the Anakites to the Nephilim as a deceptive scare tactic in order to convince the people to kill Moses and to return to Egypt. However, their report was not credible then, and it is not credible now. In fact, hours after giving their ominous report, all ten spies died of a mysterious plague, prompting the people to erroneously put their undivided energies into pursuing God's purpose their own way.[2]

Almost forty years later when Joshua entered the land of Canaan, he met and defeated most of the Anakites, but he never faced any half-angel, half-humans. The only "Spirit being" in human form that Joshua encountered in the promised land was the angel that was sent by God to fight on the Israelites' behalf as the commander of the LORD's Army. Incidentally, the proponents of the Anakite theory also believe that Goliath was a descendant of the Nephilim species because he was a giant. But how did Goliath and his lineage of giants escape the flood?[3]

Jesus never mentioned half-angels, half-humans in His mission

Jesus, as the second Adam, endows the right to become sons of God to those who believe in Him while we are still alive on earth. A more serious problem with the fallen angel view, is that Jesus compared Noah's generation to our generation over two centuries after the Septuagint translators had completed their work, and He never mentioned angelic-humans as a branch of humanity that He had come to redeem (or not to redeem). Furthermore,

❑   The early church fathers who advocated for the fallen angel theory could not have known about the type of depravity in our world today that would make the twenty-first century almost identical with Noah's world. These early church leaders certainly did not imagine human cloning as a possibility.

❑ Jesus also taught that "angels are sexless," and any attempt to make the fallen angels as an exception to this rule requires additional faith to believe.

NEW TESTAMENT VERSES USED TO SUPPORT FALLEN ANGEL VIEW

Some proponents of the fallen angel viewpoint use three key passages in the New Testament as justification. We need to examine the exact wording of these passages to decipher what the original writers were trying to communicate. Since I am not a Hebrew or Greek scholar, my conclusions are based on how these Scriptures read to an average person reading the New International Version.

I Peter 3:18-20:

For Christ died for sins once for all, the righteous for the unrighteous, to bring you to God. He was put to death in the body but made alive by the Spirit, **through whom** *also he went and preached to the spirits in prison who disobeyed long ago when God waited patiently in the days of Noah while the ark was being built (emphasis mine).*

The key phrase in this passage is "through whom." The Spirit is the subject of this discussion, and Peter is referring to the power of God that raised Jesus from the dead. This does not mean that while He was in the grave Jesus went to the holding cell where the people in Noah's day were supposedly kept and preached to them (as some have interpreted this passage). Rather, it seems to me that Peter was saying that the Spirit that raised Jesus from the dead was the same Spirit that spoke through Noah.

Jude 6-7:

> *And the angels who did not keep their positions of authority but abandoned their own home—these he has kept in darkness, bound with everlasting chains for judgment on the great Day.* **In a similar way**, *Sodom and Gomorrah and the surrounding towns gave themselves up to sexual immorality and perversion. They serve as an example of those who suffer the punishment of eternal fire (emphasis mine).*

In this passage, Jude is comparing two separate events based on their common "judgment" or outcomes. In one case there was a sentence but the judgment was delayed, making fallen angels princes of the air. In the other case, judgment and sentence were instantaneous, causing Sodom and Gomorrah to be incinerated.

When Satan was sentenced to hell, all the other angelic beings that had joined his conspiracy also went with him. Having lived in God's glorious light, anything short of it would be complete darkness. These fallen angels were removed from the glorious presence of the Most High God and are bound to a God-ordained limitation of what they can and cannot do. The fall of these angelic beings was a direct result of their refusal to function within the boundaries of their creation. Jude was saying that in a similar manner, the people in Sodom and Gomorrah had abandoned part of their mandate for living mission, and they had become complacent in their prosperity and in the way they treated each other. While their homosexuality was an aberration of God's design, God considered their mistreatment of strangers an equivalent sin.

Comparing Sodom and Gomorrah's homosexual lifestyle to sexual intercourse between fallen angels and human women is like comparing apples to oranges. While the homosexuals in Sodom and

Gomorrah could not reproduce their kind, the sexual perversity in Noah's day led to the birth of the Nephilim, and this was the reason God decided to destroy the world.

Sodom and Gomorrah were destroyed not only because of their homosexuality but also because they had become so arrogant in their prosperity that they neglected those in need around them.[4] To imply that the people in Sodom and Gomorrah knew that the two strangers they tried to rape in Lot's house were actual angels is a stretch. Not even Abraham, who was a friend of God and the beneficiary of God's personal visit, was initially aware that the three men who were wandering outside of his tent were divine beings. It was much later, as Abraham entertained them, that he realized these were no ordinary men.[5] In short, the destruction of Sodom had already been planned before the two angels arrived at Lot's house.

2 Peter 2:4-9:

For **if God did not spare angels when they sinned**, *but sent them to hell, putting them into gloomy dungeons to be held for judgment;* **if he did not spare the ancient world** *when he* brought the flood on its ungodly people, *but protected Noah, a preacher of* *righteousness, and seven others;* **if he condemned the cities of Sodom and Gomorrah** *by burning them to ashes, and made them an example of what is going to happen to the ungodly; and* **if he rescued Lot***, a righteous man, who was distressed by the filthy lives of lawless men (for that righteous man, living among them day after day, was tormented in his righteous soul by the lawless deeds he saw and heard)—***if this is so, then** *the Lord knows how to rescue godly men from trials and to hold the unrighteous for the day of judgment, while continuing their punishment (emphasis mine).*

The key phrase is "if this is so, then." Peter was comparing God's punishment of the unrighteous to His deliverance of the righteous in three separate events. The only common thread that ties these events together is God's sovereignty over all of life. While God is patient with those who refuse to fulfill His purpose for creation, He eventually moves in righteous judgment to guarantee that His intended purposes for creation come to fruition.

In each of the events referred to above, the righteous were delivered because they acted within the confines of their created purposes and because of their good deeds. On the other hand, the unrighteous were judged on the basis of their refusal to act within the confines of their created order or purposes and because of their evil actions. This passage is an excellent comparison of separate events with a predictable blissful outcome and the other with a miserable outcome. There is no suggestion here that angelic beings had sexual relations with women and produced angelic-human offspring.

What all three passages have in common is that the distinction is made between godliness and ungodliness: obedience versus disobedience, righteous living versus unrighteous living—heaven for the righteous and hell for the unrighteous. There were godly angels and ungodly angels, righteous angels and unrighteous angels. There were angels who tried to become what they were not made to be, and there were angels who remained faithful to their created purpose. In similar fashion, there are godly humans and ungodly humans. There are humans who disobediently want to live outside the boundaries of God-established gender order and those who obediently abide by it. There are humans who want to live without God and function outside the parameters of mankind's mandate for living, and there are those who love God and hold to the tenets of the mandate.

Noah's world was destroyed because unrighteousness was demonstrated by the presence of the Nephilim—monstrous creatures born of the mixture of the sons of God with the sons of men. Why would a righteous God allow such a grotesque species to infiltrate human beings which He formed in His own image and likeness? It was this difficulty in explaining how fallen angels could have had sex with human women that led some early church fathers to conclude that the "sons of God" were the descendants of Seth and that the "daughters of men" were the descendants of Cain.

THE SETHITE VIEW

Historians, like Josephus and Philo, and some early church fathers, like Justin and Eusebius, held to the "fallen angel theory" until this view was challenged by some backslidden Christians, like Celsus and Julian the Apostate, who questioned the truth of the myth of half-angel, half-human creatures. During the fifth century, Julius Africanus (a contemporary of Origen) theorized that the "sons of God" were the descendants of Seth, because they were committed to preserving the worship of God.

Other early church thinkers, like Chrysostom and Augustine, also supported this Sethite view of the sons of God.

The Sethite school of thought is even more difficult to defend than the fallen angel view. The Bible clearly separates the descendants of Cain from those of Seth. The descendants of Seth were known as the sons of men, because Seth was the first human born in the fully mortal human image and likeness of Adam. It is also impossible to substantiate the view that the descendants of Seth were all God-fearing people.

Furthermore, when the sons of men married the daughters of men, they produced sons and daughters of men, not giant grotesque offspring. Some within the Sethite school of thought explained this discrepancy by claiming that the daughters of men were the descendants of Cain (the ungodly ones). This view not only distorts Scripture, but it depicts women as universally evil by virtue of their gender. The Nephilim passage clearly identifies the origin of the daughters of men: "When men began to increase in number on the earth and daughters were born to them..."

So, for those who believe that the sons of God were fallen angels: if the sons and daughters of men were descended from Seth, who then were the Cainites? And if Jesus is correct in comparing our generation to Noah's generation, why is it that we do not see giant half-angel, half-humans roaming the world today? Only humanity and all living creatures have been endowed with the ability to procreate their kind—a mandate that excludes all angels—fallen or not. While fallen angels are spirits and can inhabit humans, they are not creator spirits; and therefore, cannot reproduce themselves either in their kind by birthing other angels, or by mixing with mankind. If the sons of God were neither the descendants of Seth nor fallen angels, who were they?

Note:
1. See Deuteronomy 1:28; 2:21; 9:2; Joshua 11:21;14:12,15; 15:14.
2. Numbers 14.
3. Goliath was no more a Nephilim than Shaquille O'Neil (the over seven foot tall basketball star) is one. While both Goliath and Shaq are giants of men, they are human beings, not half-angels.
4. Ezekiel 16:49-50.
5. Genesis 18:1-8.

Chapter 3

WHO WERE THE SONS OF GOD?

Based on Scriptural evidence alone, the Nephilim were the offspring of the union between the sons of God and the daughters of men. In order to understand the Nephilim, we must first correctly decipher who the sons of God were and how they originated. To decipher who the sons of God were, we need to go back to the beginning of time.

Angels are often referred to in Scripture as the sons of God (Bene Elohim) because they were created as spirit beings. Angels are able to dwell in the Presence of the Lord, or in the case of the fallen angels, to appear before that Presence, and they are able to take human form when they are on special assignments to mankind. However, because angels were not created in the image and likeness of God, they do not have the ability to procreate beings like themselves or to mix their genes with any other form.

Adam was created in the image and likeness of God, making him the first human "son of God." This applies to all his offspring as well. This means that Adam was a spirit being in human flesh. Eve, who was formed by God from Adam's rib, was also a spirit being with the same capabilities as Adam. Adam and Eve were given the charter to procreate their kind and to live and work as God's representatives, first in the Garden of Eden and then throughout the earth. Because of their God-nature, Adam and Eve were able to appear in person before the Presence of the LORD for daily fellowship and worship.

Figure 3-1

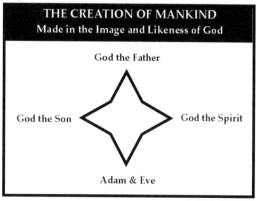

THE CREATION OF MANKIND
Made in the Image and Likeness of God

God the Father

God the Son   God the Spirit

Adam & Eve

In essence, Adam's and Eve's bodies were not subject to electromagnetic and gravitational forces, which allowed them to move between the earthly and spiritual realms. Jesus Christ demonstrated this phenomenon when He transfigured into the heavenlies, where He had a strategic meeting with Moses and Elijah, while His trembling disciples Peter, James, and John looked on in awe.

When Adam and Eve sinned by eating the forbidden fruit, they short-circuited their God-nature, and thus their ability to appear before the Presence of the LORD. They destroyed their ability to live eternally. Since they failed to appear before God's Presence, God came looking for them in the Garden of Eden, where they were hiding behind bushes.[1]

God made several attempts to help His beleaguered favorites repent of their disobedient act and to receive His mercy, but Adam and Eve turned every such opportunity down. Since they refused to take responsibility for their actions, God sacrificed a substitute animal on their behalf so that they could appear before His Presence. God used the skin from the animal to clothe Adam and Eve, to give them more time to recognize the futility of their lives without God, and to turn back around toward following God's plan and purposes for His world.[2]

After this solemn ceremony demonstrating God's infinite grace and mercy, Adam and Eve were banished from their garden paradise to serve out their sentence on earth. God said at the time, "The man has now become like one of us, knowing good and evil. He must not be allowed to reach out his hand and take also from the tree of life and eat, and live forever."[3]

Adam and Eve's banishment did not immediately keep them from continuing to exist as spirit beings, but their judgment did prevent them from coming into the Presence of God until the time of their physical deaths. The most immediate consequence of their fall was that they no longer had access to the tree of life which was in the Garden of Eden. Their judgment required them to eventually experience physical death, a sort of shedding off or purging from the corrupted Adamic nature. Since God had already made the atonement sacrifice for them, Adam and Eve had only to undergo physical death before they could again have access to the tree of life, and in that process obtain eternal life in the everlasting Presence of God in the highest heavens.

Figure 3-2

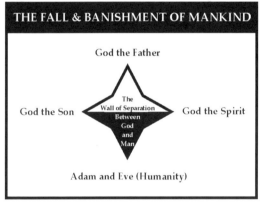

THE FALL & BANISHMENT OF MANKIND

God the Father

The Wall of Separation Between God and Man

God the Son   God the Spirit

Adam and Eve (Humanity)

The first human offspring

When Adam and Eve gave birth to Cain and Abel, the first couple were still functioning as spirit-born human beings. Eve was certain at that time that her first offspring would prove to be the Divine Child, or Seed, who would crush Satan's head.[4] Eve knew that she was destined to experience severe pain during childbirth because that was woman's judgment for the fall. The birth of the first human offspring was achieved by both a supernatural means and by a natural process. For this reason, Eve named her first son Cain, which means: "I have acquired a man from the LORD."[5] In other words, "I have acquired a son of God." By the time their second child was born, the effect of their disobedience was becoming more manifest in their Adamic nature (body and soul). Hence, the birth of Abel occurred more by natural process and less by supernatural means. This is probably why the first couple named their second son Abel, which means "frail." While Eve was right to claim she had acquired a son of God, she was wrong in assuming that Cain was the promised Divine Seed, since Adam had provided the sperm (DNA) for both Cain and Abel's conception.

Cain and Abel were the sons of God (Bene Elohim), not because of anything they would do, but by virtue of Adam's God-imbued Spirit, which Adam had received at creation and was still very much alive in him when Cain and Abel were conceived and born. The descendants of Cain (Cainites) and all the other human beings born to Adam and Eve before Seth inherited their birthright status as sons of God because Adam, their father, was at the time of their conception a human "spirit being."

Figure 3-3

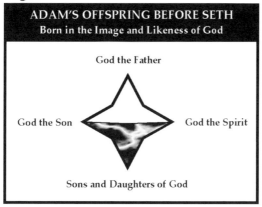

To further support this position, neither Adam nor any of his offspring (before Seth) had a date of birth, and of these only Adam had a date of death. This is because spirit beings are supernatural beings and do not have a natural lifespan.

When Adam compromised his wholeness in God by eating the forbidden fruit, he effectively compromised the sanctity of his seed and future offspring—mankind. Hence, both Cain and Abel inherited the Adamic sinful nature as well as Adam's spirit-nature, from their parents. Because of the first couple's sin of disobedience, all human beings were sentenced to die, before they could inherit eternal life. In essence, although the sons of God were born in God's nature (which is eternal), they also inherited a judgment that had to be atoned for before they could live forever in God's Presence. This was the reason Cain and Abel were required to bring the substitution sacrifice even though they had temporary access into the Presence of God through the spirit-nature they had inherited from Adam.

The extinction of sons of God (Cainites)

When Cain and Abel brought their sacrifice to God, Abel's offering was accepted because it was a blood sacrifice—the same kind of sacrifice God had made on behalf of Adam and Eve before He banished them. But Cain brought fruits as an offering for atonement, so his sacrifice was rejected.

Despite God's appeal to Cain to do the right thing by bringing the right kind of sacrifice, Cain rejected God's counsel. Eventually he killed his brother, Abel. Although Cain succeeded in killing Abel's physical body, he could not take away the eternal life that Abel had obtained by obedience to God. It was this first murder in the history of humanity that earned Cain and his descendants the sentence of physical extinction from the natural element (human bodies) of their supernatural being. The premature physical death that Cain inflicted on Abel became the root of his own judgment.

God proclaimed at Cain's sentencing: "Now you are under a curse and driven from the ground, which opened its mouth to receive your brother's blood from your hand. When you work the ground, it will no longer yield its crops for you. You will be a restless wanderer on the earth."[6] Cain understood his sentence to mean immediate death at the hands of his relatives or some other living creatures. (According to ancient traditions, Adam and Eve continued to have children who were all part of the lineage of the sons of God—until Seth was born.)

Through God's clarification of what would happen to the person who committed the next murder, we can decipher the timeline for the full manifestation of Cain's curse. God revealed the mystery of His judgment on Cain when He declared, "… if anyone kills Cain, he will suffer vengeance seven times over."[7] The punishment that Cain's murderer would receive was in line with the punishment that Cain received for Abel's murder.

The lineage of the sons of God was now destined to become extinct at the end of the seventh generation. Adam and Eve's judgment affected all of their offspring perpetually, but Cain's lineage—the human sons of God—would also be under the curse God placed on Cain. Because of the sentence of extinction now placed on the sons of God, Adam and Eve faced the possibility that they might never fulfill mankind's mandate: "Be fruitful and increase in number; fill the earth and subdue it. Rule over the fish of the sea and the birds of the air and over every living creature that moves on the ground."[8]

The origin of the sons of men

Since God had a divine purpose when He created man, nothing could stop His plans from coming to fruition. In His infinite wisdom, love, and mercy, God allowed Adam to slowly become completely mortal before he could begin a new lineage of humanity. By the time of Seth's conception, Adam had fully reverted to his mortal or human nature[9]:

> When God created man, he made him in the likeness of God. He created them male and female and blessed them. And when they were created, he called them 'man.' When Adam had lived 130 years, he had a son in his own likeness, in his own image; and he named him Seth....Adam lay with his wife again, and she gave birth to a son and named him Seth, saying, "God has granted me another child in place of Abel, since Cain killed him." Seth also had a son, and he named him Enosh. At that time men began to call on the name of the LORD.

It was because Adam had become completely mortal that his years of existence were converted to a mortal timeline, and his age was recorded as 130 years. The birth of Seth began a new natural human race that was no longer a supernatural "spirit born" human species as the offspring of Cain and of Adam and Eve's other children had been. Instead, for the first time in history, human beings began to call on the name of the LORD rather than simply transfiguring into His Presence. As a result, two human species roamed the earth—the sons of God (Cainites) and the sons of men (Sethites).

Figure 3-4

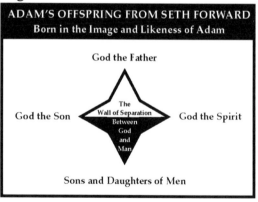

ADAM'S OFFSPRING FROM SETH FORWARD
Born in the Image and Likeness of Adam

God the Father

The Wall of Separation Between God and Man

God the Son

God the Spirit

Sons and Daughters of Men

Some biblical scholars have a problem calling the line of Cain "the sons of God," because of the sins that this line introduced to humanity. Cainites earned their status as human sons of God by birthright—not because of their future actions, but because they were direct descendants of the spirit-being-in-human-flesh Adam. However, the Cainites' status as sons of God did not automatically earn them eternal life, since they shared (by virtue of the same birthright) in Adam's sin which resulted in mortality.

The extinction of the sons of God by the seventh generation was to have left only the sons of men on earth. This may explain why God put a mark on Cain, so no one who found him would kill him. If Seth had killed Cain, for instance, then the whole lineage of the sons of men would also have been scheduled for extinction by the seventh generation. This is why the Cainites as a species were separated from the Sethites and sent to a place called Nod to begin the process of the extinction of their human nature. The mark was also a counter or reference point for the beginning (Cain) and the end (seventh generation) of the curse. The death of the Cainites came by supernatural means, since they were not fully mortal. As God's judgment took effect on the line of Cain, these beings began to die out while Adam their father was still alive, until the sixth generation, during the time of Lamech, when Adam himself died.

Lamech, knowing that his offspring were scheduled to be the last to die for the murder of Abel, tried to circumvent the curse by marrying two women, Adah and Zillah, from the sons of men lineage (Seth's descendants), thus producing offspring that would be partly the sons of God (destined for extinction) and partly the sons of men (destined to fulfill mankind's mandate for living). Lamech's offspring became the seventh generation of the sons of God and the first generation of the Nephilim species.

WHAT JESUS TAUGHT ABOUT THE SUPERNATURAL AND NATURAL WORLDS

As the only human being (since Adam) to be conceived without the contribution of man (the Adamic nature), Jesus' death on the cross became the one permanent sacrifice that had been promised from the time of the fall of Adam and Eve. Since every person alive today is born in the Adamic nature, we all share in the Adamic sin and from birth are estranged from God. Accepting Jesus Christ as the substitute sacrifice reconnects us back to God eternally and puts us at the table of goodness where the triune God communes.

Before His death and resurrection, Jesus makes this point about what it takes to be reborn into a Spirit-being while conversing with the high-ranking Jewish teacher Nicodemus. He stated that, "Flesh gives birth to flesh, but the Spirit gives birth to the spirit."[10] When pressed for clarity by Nicodemus, Jesus revealed His authority as a member of the triune God by declaring: "I tell you the truth, we speak of what we know, and we testify to what we have seen, but still you people do not accept our testimony. I have spoken to you of earthly things and you do not believe; how then will you believe if I speak of heavenly things? No one has ever gone into heaven except the one who came from heaven—the Son of Man."[11]

Ironically, Jesus never mentioned the Nephilim as angelic-humans in any of His discourses, nor did He include them as part of His mission. Not even during His dialogue with Nicodemus, when it would have been most relevant, did Jesus mention another species of mankind. From this, we can conclude that angelic-humans never existed as a human species.

Is there life after death?

After the fall, the biggest difference between supernatural beings and natural beings remains in the areas of the attainment of eternal life and obtaining access to the spiritual world. On another occasion, a group of religious scholars (Sadducees) came to Jesus to inquire about the existence of life after death (eternal life) and the relationships between men and women on the other side of the pearly gates (heaven). On the issue of gender relationships, Jesus responded:

> *The sons of this age do marry and are given in marriage, but those accounted worthy to obtain that age, and the rising again that is out of the dead, neither marry, nor are they given in marriage; for neither are they able to die any more—for they are like messengers—and they are sons of God, being sons of the rising again.*[12]

Regarding the existence of life after death, Jesus responded:

> *Now that the dead are raised, even Moses showed at the bush when he called the Lord `the God of Abraham and the God of Isaac and the God of Jacob.' For He is not a God of the dead, but of the living, for all live unto Him.*[13]

The scholars who brought these questions to Jesus were satisfied with His answers two thousand years ago—they went away saying, "Well said, teacher."[14] This statement along with Jesus' remarks about the nature of Noah's world when they were "… marrying and giving in marriage"[15] ought to have settled the debate about whether fallen angels and human women could come together to produce angelic-human offspring.

When Jesus died on the cross two thousand years ago, He bridged the Wall of Separation between God and man that had existed since the time of Adam and Eve's banishment. The new sons and daughters of God are those who have been born again by the same Spirit that raised Jesus (the second Adam) from the dead. The right to become a "son or daughter of God" today is not a birthright, but an inheritance that was paid for by the blood of Christ and must be freely accepted as a gift. This is why the theology that the Nephilim were a hybrid of fallen angels and humans leaves so many unanswerable questions. If our generation is similar to the generation of Noah, where are the angelic-humans today? How does one physically differentiate the sons of God fathered by fallen angels roaming the earth from the sons and daughters of God that have been redeemed by the shed blood of Christ and reconciled to God?

Figure 3-5

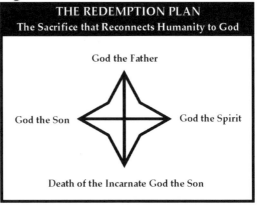

THE REDEMPTION PLAN
The Sacrifice that Reconnects Humanity to God

God the Father

God the Son

God the Spirit

Death of the Incarnate God the Son

Figure 3-6

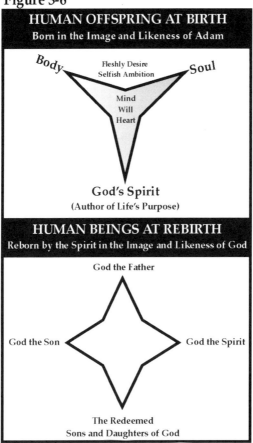

HUMAN OFFSPRING AT BIRTH
Born in the Image and Likeness of Adam

Body

Fleshly Desire
Selfish Ambition

Soul

Mind
Will
Heart

God's Spirit
(Author of Life's Purpose)

HUMAN BEINGS AT REBIRTH
Reborn by the Spirit in the Image and Likeness of God

God the Father

God the Son

God the Spirit

The Redeemed
Sons and Daughters of God

Notes:
1. Genesis 3:8.
2. Genesis 3:21.
3. Genesis 3:22.
4. Genesis 3:15.
5. Genesis 4:1, NKJV.
6. Genesis 4:11-12.
7. Genesis 4:15.
8. Genesis 1:28.
9. Genesis 5:1-3;   4:25-26.
10. John 3:6.
11. John 3:11-13.
12. Luke 20:34-36 (Young's Literal Translation).
13. Luke 20:37-38 (KJ21).
14. Luke 20:39.
15. Matthew 24:38.

Chapter 4

DE-MYSTIFYING THE NEPHILIM WORLD

The Nephilim story has caused much confusion in our understanding of the real issues leading to Noah's flood. Yet, in light of the fact that Jesus compared the events leading to His Second Coming to the events that led to the destruction of Noah's world, it is vital that we understand who the Nephilim were and why they had such a devastating influence. To unlock the mysteries and fully understand the Nephilim and the period in which they existed, we need three keys:

❑ We need to be guided by the Holy Spirit and to be willing to interpret Scriptures through His paradigm or window.

❑   We need to employ project management techniques in order to understand the timeline for when and how the Nephilim came into existence, what they did wrong, and why they were obliterated from God's world.

❑   We need to accept the Nephilim phenomenon as a form of human cloning— something that is feasible now for the first time since Noah's flood.

THE FIRST HUMAN CLONES

Genesis 6:4 reads:

> *The Nephilim were on the earth in those days—and also afterward—when the sons of God went to the daughters of men and had children by them. They were the heroes of old, men of renown.*

This reference to the Nephilim in Scripture, unlike other passages, could not have been fully understood in any era of humanity until recent times, when we face the real possibility of the presence on earth of two human species—one that goes back to Noah and the other that comes out of a petri dish (laboratory). The above passage about the Nephilim not only demonstrates the relevance today of Scriptures, but makes explicit how precisely the information it contains applies to modern mankind.

In Noah's era, when the sons of men were increasing in number, a son of man who married a daughter of God (assuming they still existed) would have automatically committed himself to not fathering a lineage because the daughters of God were under the extinction curse of Cain.

Cainites—under the curse of extinction—had every reason to want to clone themselves by marrying the daughters of men. This would enable them to produce offspring that would keep their lineage alive forever and thus circumvent the curse. Judging from the genealogy of the purebred sons of God, Lamech seemed to have been the last one alive, except for Adam (who had already reverted back to his Adamic nature). But Lamech, who was the last known member of the sons of God species, married two women, and this fact provides us with an important clue to the origin of the Nephilim.

Since we know more about the Nephilim children of Lamech than about any others of this new breed of humanity, we can look to them to provide us with clues as to how to decipher the Nephilim myth. Lamech's offspring, as far as we know, were the first Nephilim, and by the magnitude of their accomplishments they defined the Nephilim sub-culture and world order.

Nephilim—the fallen ones, heroes of old, and men of renown

The Nephilim species was the third human species to inhabit the earth, and they had no God-defined purpose for existing. Since as spirit-born human beings the sons of God had no date of birth or date of death, their clones—the Nephilim—did not have these either, because they were an extension of their fathers' lives. The Nephilim existed as half-mortal, half-immortal remnants from the ancient sons of God stock, making them the heroes of old. The fact that the Nephilim were mortals meant that they were subject to gravity. This earned them the title "the fallen ones" since they could not move between the physical and spiritual worlds as their fathers had. Since Lamech was the sixth generation son of God, once his cloned offspring were on earth, it made no difference whether he was physically alive or dead. Through his Nephilim offspring, Lamech hoped to gain eternal life and secure the posterity of the sons of God on earth while he and his fathers wandered as spirits in the afterlife in conformity to God's decree. Hence the terms "Nephilim" and "sons of God" became synonymous.

In order to survive in this diabolical world, the Nephilim became the first nihilists. Nihilism, according to the Merriam-Webster dictionary, is "a viewpoint that traditional values and beliefs are unfounded and that existence is senseless and useless….a doctrine that denies any objective ground of truth and especially of moral truths."

Beginning with the three sons of Lamech (Jabal, Jubal, and Tubal-Cain), the Nephilim created their own nihilistic worldview. Lamech's three sons introduced three key professions to mankind, and these professions were the seeds of the agricultural, the informational, and the industrial ages. Jabal, as the father of nomadic shepherding, invented the service industry of the day and controlled the livestock markets. Jubal became the father of the entertainment industry when he invented various ways to score music and to play the harp and flute.

Tubal-Cain became the father of the manufacturing industry when he invented ways to forge tools out of bronze and iron.[1] According to the historian Josephus, Tubal-Cain was also an expert in martial arts and body building—the foundation of holistic health and alternative health care. These key revolutions gave the Nephilim control over the socio-cultural, economic, and political infrastructure of God's second world order[2] and thus gained great status with the sons of men. This established the Nephilim as "the heroes of old and the men of renown":

- ❑ Nomadic shepherding was the Nephilim's attempt to render the curse of "restless wanderings" beneficial and productive. Inventing this service industry guaranteed the Nephilim a continued food supply and provided them with consistent trading commodities (currency).
- ❑ Scoring music for the harp and flute was the Nephilim's attempt to subvert the curse that the sons of God would not "fill the earth" with their own creations. Inventing the

entertainment industry guaranteed the human clones the information platform to preserve and propagate their sons-of-God heritage, thus guaranteeing their own posterity.

❑ Forging metal and bronze into tools was the Nephilim's attempt to subvert the curse on the sons of God that they would not be part of the human stream that "subdues the earth." The manufacturing industry that the human clones invented allowed them to forge tools for tilling the earth, guaranteeing that the ground would always "yield its crops." They may have also created tools that allowed them to artificially "rule over the fish, the birds, and every living creature that moved along the ground" including the sons of men.

Only the children of Lamech and their descendants could have qualified as Nephilim, the "heroes of old" and as "men of renown." They would also have qualified as "giants," because of their unusual height due to their genetic combinations. In a similar fashion, animal cloning in our day has resulted in giant or oversized creatures, validating (by association) the Scriptural claims that the Nephilim were giants.

The execution of Lamech's curse

Lamech's attempt to circumvent God's judgment by means of human cloning quickly backfired when he killed a young man in a random skirmish. This second act of murder in human history guaranteed the extinction of the human-sons of God clones that Lamech had just introduced into God's world order. True to God's judgment proclaimed on the lineage of Cain, Lamech's offspring became the last known original clones of the sons of God. See Table 4-2. Every other human clone from this point forward was a clone of a clone, and because of Lamech's murder they too were marked for extinction[3]:

> When men began to increase in number on the earth
> and daughters were born to them, the sons of God saw that
> the daughters of men were beautiful, and they married any
> of them they chose. Then the LORD said, "My Spirit will
> not contend with man forever, for he is mortal; his days will
> be a hundred and twenty years."

From this passage we can surmise that the only stream of humanity whose population was growing exponentially was the lineage of Seth. The question of the ages is why the sons of God were marrying the daughters of men when there is no equivalent mention of the daughters of God marrying the sons of men. The answer to this question lies in the fact that females hold the keys to natural human reproduction because they are the only ones who can produce the eggs needed for conception to occur.

As sons of God, the Cainites knew that if the daughters of God were no longer producing the eggs needed to procreate their kind, mixing their seed with the daughters of men (who had no problems with human egg production, judging from their rapidly expanding population) would give them the offspring they needed to continue to exist in human form forever, in defiance of God's purpose for His world. Conversely, if the sons of men had married the daughters of God (assuming they existed and there were enough of them to go around), they would not have been able to multiply their sons-of-men kind, since the daughters of God would also have been under the curse of extinction and therefore infertile. Is it possible that for every one of the Nephilim that survived, many died prematurely because of Cain's sentence that came into full effect beginning with Lamech's offspring?

Timeline for the existence of the Nephilim

With the continued existence of Lamech's Nephilim children, it appeared as though the sons of God succeeded in thwarting God's plan to wipe them out. This is why I also believe that the passage in Genesis 6 that describes the Nephilim gives us two critical timelines to use in determining the period of their origination and their extinction. "The Nephilim were on the earth in those days," refers back to the time of the first human clones (when Lamech's offspring should have been the last expression of the gene pool of the sons of God) until the time Noah was called to build an ark to prepare for the impending deluge. During this period, human clones increased in number, and thus kept the stream of the sons of God alive. "… and afterwards" refers to the 120 years of God's grace period, during which Noah built the ark and preached the message of righteousness to his generation before the flood.

Figure 4-1

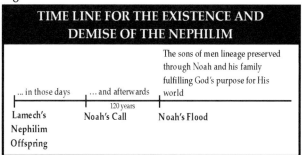

Interestingly, between the time Methuselah was born, starting the counter for the extinction of the Nephilim species (around 3313 B. C.), and the time when Noah was called to build the ark (around 2464 B.C.), eight hundred and forty-nine years passed. During this period, many streams of the sons of God clones roamed the earth, even as they celebrated their human successes and rejoiced that they had beaten the curse of extinction.

Figure 4-2

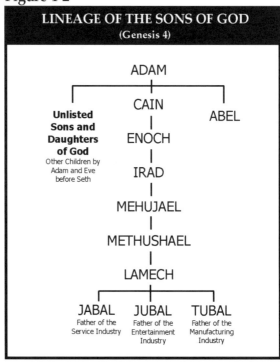

LINEAGE OF THE SONS OF GOD
(Genesis 4)

ADAM

Unlisted Sons and Daughters of God
Other Children by Adam and Eve before Seth

CAIN

ABEL

ENOCH

IRAD

MEHUJAEL

METHUSHAEL

LAMECH

JABAL
Father of the Service Industry

JUBAL
Father of the Entertainment Industry

TUBAL
Father of the Manufacturing Industry

Figure 4-3

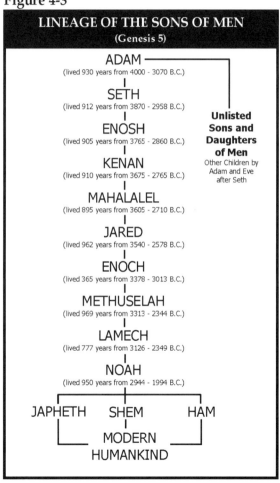

LINEAGE OF THE SONS OF MEN
(Genesis 5)

ADAM
(lived 930 years from 4000 - 3070 B.C.)

SETH
(lived 912 years from 3870 - 2958 B.C.)

ENOSH
(lived 905 years from 3765 - 2860 B.C.)

KENAN
(lived 910 years from 3675 - 2765 B.C.)

MAHALALEL
(lived 895 years from 3605 - 2710 B.C.)

JARED
(lived 962 years from 3540 - 2578 B.C.)

ENOCH
(lived 365 years from 3378 - 3013 B.C.)

METHUSELAH
(lived 969 years from 3313 - 2344 B.C.)

LAMECH
(lived 777 years from 3126 - 2349 B.C.)

NOAH
(lived 950 years from 2944 - 1994 B.C.)

JAPHETH   SHEM   HAM

MODERN
HUMANKIND

Unlisted Sons and Daughters of Men
Other Children by Adam and Eve after Seth

To mankind in this era, God had become obsolete and His purpose for His world, irrelevant. As time passed and as the Nephilim sons of God increased, so did the grotesque appearance of their offspring. A son of God clone, married to another clone, gave birth to a different kind of creature. A third generation clone, married to a daughter of men, produced another stream of the sons of God.

Notes:

1. Genesis 4:20-22.
2. God's second world order is the period after the fall and before the flood.
3. Genesis 4:17-22; Genesis 6:1-3.

Chapter 5

THE INCARNATION
AND HUMAN CLONING

God's Creation revealed in human diversity is one of the wonders of our world. While there are approximately 6.2 billion people in the world today, no two people are exactly alike—not even members of the same family, not even identical twins. What is more fascinating about God's creativity is that even though no two people are identical, we all share in the genetic pool of Noah and his wife, no matter where we came from or in what generation we were born or what color of skin we adorn.

Four thousand years after the sentencing of Adam and Eve, the Divine Seed, whose assignment it was to provide the way back to humanity's lost paradise, arrived and fulfilled His role and responsibilities. While the Incarnation of the Son of God was a phenomenon that for a long time did not fit into the scientific worldview, through the possibility of human cloning, scientists may have also stumbled into facts supporting it. Interestingly, four thousand years after the destruction of the first world order that had succeeded in cloning human beings, this generation of humanity is back to repeating human cloning as though it were a new phenomenon.

Since the result of the first human cloning phenomenon adversely affected everyone living in Noah's day, the advent of human cloning in the twenty-first century has the same potential to alter the destiny of humanity as we know it. Therefore, it is paramount that the public square debate about proceeding with any form of human cloning or about dealing with the aftermath of a world with human clones must include the ethical, religious, societal, scientific, and medical implications. So far, the scientific and medical communities have led the movement and shaped the dialogue toward human cloning. While the religious communities have registered some opposition, the global media has feasted on the potential of this incredible biomedical breakthrough, and much of humanity has remained oblivious as to what role it must play. Furthermore, much of the discussion on all sides already engaged in the public square debate has centered on the unknown future of human cloning and not on the known world of human cloning during Noah's time.

Ironically, the same Bible that many within the scientific community pass over as irrelevant and out-of-date has the very answers to what scientists are postulating now as the possible effects of cloning on human clones. Albeit Einstein said it best: "Science without religion is lame, religion without science is blind." We need both science and religion to make sense of human cloning and to respond appropriately.

Since any attempt at human cloning is a direct challenge at modifying God's creation, it only makes sense for us to expect that He will respond to such a challenge as He did in times past. And like in Noah's time, everyone alive in the twenty-first century will be impacted by God's decision. This is all the more reason why it would be a travesty to celebrate the advent of human cloning and fail to let the rest of the world know the expected divine outcome of this human achievement. All stakeholders (humanity in general) must have access to information concerning the pros and cons of human cloning, and their voices and concerns must be heard and taken into consideration by those who would make this phenomenon a reality.

For most people though, the idea of getting involved in an issue that is so technical and that has its own communication language can become intimidating. However, the language of the "scientific street" regarding human cloning is not as complicated as it sounds when we find common everyday concepts that relate to the scientific and medical terminologies. In the discussions following, this book attempts to level the "playing field" of our general understanding.

A person is made of cells, which are like working units (groups) within the person. All the instructions needed for these cells to operate are contained within a chemical formulation known as DNA. Every person's DNA consists of the same chemical and physical components, and each person's complete set of DNA is known as his or her genome. For example, the working cells in your hands that allow you to make a hand motion is equally present in every other human being, who can also make the same motion with their own unique variation. However, that does not mean that the cells in your hand can only do hand motions.

DNA is the basis for a person's genes, which contain the basic physical and functional units of heredity. Scientists have discovered that each person has about 3.2 billion pairs of chemicals that form from 35,000 and 45,000 genes. Compare the 3.2 billion pairs of chemicals that form your genes to your home's light switch, which has two functions— on and off. When you flip your light switch on, it may be represented as 1, and when you turn it off as 0. Every time you flip your light switch on or off, think of your action as performing "1" and "0" functions. Depending on how many times a day you do this routine, we could represent your actions as 1010 or 0101.

Although, each human being may have the same number of pairs of chemicals or DNA, the randomness of how each gene combination of pairs (1's and 0's) is turned on or off in certain places determines our uniqueness from other human beings. This simple "1's and 0's" analogy is the basis for the computer programs that run your word processing software or play your movies. Whether you are using your computer to type a document or to watch a movie, the programming code behind your experience is just executing "1's and 0's." While one set of the "1's and 0's" routines (combination) displays the typed phrase "beauty and the beast" another set plays the movie "Beauty and the Beast."

On April 14, 2003, an International Consortium of Scientists announced to the world that it had successfully mapped the human genome to an accuracy of 99.99 percent. The reason researchers could not reach 100 percent accuracy is that there is not a person alive today who is one hundred percent identical to another person. Remember Eve? Although Eve was made from Adam's rib (his DNA), she was still different from him because of the sequence of what God turned on and off in her genome.

THE INCARNATION OF GOD

According to the Merriam Webster dictionary, "incarnation" is the "the embodiment of a deity or spirit in some earthly form." Before there was even a scientific concept of human cloning, God Himself revealed His Master plan to take on an earthly or mortal form after the fall in order to fulfill His purpose. God the Son was going to be born into the world as a Seed from the woman who would crush Satan's head and redeem mankind. This Divine Seed, or Child, would be conceived without the DNA or genetic contribution from a man, and there is no better way to demonstrate this than to have a virgin girl be the mother. Hence, God the Son, in human flesh, became the Incarnate Son of God, conceived by the Spirit of God (the DNA of God) using the egg of a virgin woman (Mary).

Figure 5-1

The first advent of human cloning: A counterfeit of the incarnation of God

Back in Noah's day, every single human being was a unique person. The sons of God and the sons of men were very much part of God's nature, but they were also different streams or species of that nature. When Adam was banished, the greatest manifestation of God's judgment on him (besides his eventual death) was having a son in his own image and likeness, indicating his full return back to his human nature from his original Spirit-nature. In other words, Adam and Eve were grounded on earth and were eventually denied the ability to be everywhere at the same time, a function that was possible because of their Spirit nature. In His Righteousness, God granted the first offspring of Adam and Eve (the sons of God), the same Spirit nature, enabling them to transcend, among other things, electromagnetic and gravitational forces. By the time Seth was conceived, Adam and Eve's Spirit nature was completely dimmed (muted).

Although Seth was born in the image and likeness of Adam, he was still a unique person, not a copy of Adam. By way of comparison, when Cain was judged for killing Abel, the greatest manifestation of God's curse on him was that by the seventh generation, his lineage would be extinct from the face of the earth. Using our "1's and 0's" analogy, it becomes obvious that in His Infinite Creative Wisdom, God turned off the Spirit Nature ("1's and 0's") in Seth's genome, effectively grounding him and his lineage. In essence, when Seth was conceived, God created a human clone in the new nature of Adam, without the ability to transcend electromagnetic and gravitational forces.

Although the lineages of both Cain and Seth were human, Cainites were vastly superior beings because they existed in the fullness of their Spirit and Adamic natures, making their gene pool different from the Sethites' gene pool.

God's plan, as embedded in the Garden of Eden judgment, was for God the Son to be born in human flesh, becoming the "Only Son of God-Son of Man Being" to re-ignite the Spirit nature of humanity in order to pursue God's purpose. When Lamech married the two human women, his offspring were a copy of his corrupted God nature (born in the image and likeness of the sons of God), thus keeping Cain's lineage alive beyond the seventh generation. However, introducing the sons of God gene pool into the sons of men gene pool was an adulteration of God's revealed plan for the permanent redemption of humanity through His own offspring, the Incarnate Son of God. In addition, the fact that Lamech and his offspring thought that they had outsmarted God by circumventing His decree of extinction gave the sons of God a false sense of security that they would now live forever.

However, by combining the gene pool of the sons of God and the sons of men, the Nephilim offspring that resulted were disorganized and disoriented human beings with severe peculiarities. For example, because they were made up of some sets of "1's and 0's" that could transcend electromagnetic and gravitational forces and other sets that could not, the Nephilim became known as the "fallen ones." Consider an aircraft that has the right gear for lift off, but lacks any aerodynamic capabilities to stay in flight. Because such an aircraft cannot defy gravity for long, it simply crashes back to earth. This would have been the plight of the Nephilim, thus earning them the title of the "fallen ones."

HUMAN CLONING TODAY

The possibility of human cloning has become a global issue, and just about every country in the world has its body of experts and commissions dealing with it. In order to better understand the state of human cloning today and for the foreseeable future, I will turn to two organizations that are respected authorities in the global scientific and medical aspects of human cloning: the United States Academies Committee on Science, Engineering, and Public Policy (COSEPUP) and the Academies Board of Life Sciences (BLS).

COSEPUP is made up of board members from the National Academy of Sciences, National Academy of Engineering, Institute of Medicine, and National Research Council. A joint panel of both COSEPUP and BLS published a book in 2002 that I will be referring to as my source for definitions, findings, and recommendations as I relate today's quest for human cloning to the one carried out in Noah's time.

Today, by understanding the instructions encoded in each pair of genes, researchers are able to pinpoint defective genes that cause what we call diseases. Scientists also believe that by understanding the instruction manual for what makes a person human, they now have the ability to create all kinds of cures for defective parts of the human body. So, if the cells in your hands become defective, it is possible for new ones that are exact copies of your original hand cells to be manufactured (cloned) and transplanted into your body.

This understanding also gives scientists the ability to clone or to create a copy of a human being. A true clone is one that has the same genes or identical DNA as the donor that provided the DNA for its creation. Cloning is the manufacturing of a cell or organism with the same nuclear (cell) genome as another cell or organism. The same cells cloned to provide the transplant for your hands could also be used in place of a male sperm to fertilize a human egg in order to conceive a baby.

The second advent of human cloning: A counterfeit of the creation of humankind

To create Eve, God put Adam to sleep (under anesthetics), extracted one of his ribs (DNA) and closed up the incision. God then used the rib from

Adam to create Eve, and the outcome was the human female. Although Adam had been made in the image and likeness of God, he knew that he was not a member of the Trinity. So, when Adam saw Eve for the first time, he exclaimed, "This [creature] is now bone of my bones and flesh of my flesh; she shall be called Woman, because she was taken out of a man."[1] Eve came into existence by the hand of God's creativity, using the DNA of Adam, and she was wonderfully made, perfectly whole, and specifically made different from Adam.

Ironically, many in the past have questioned why Adam and all men in general don't have one less rib than women, if it is true that Adam did loose a rib. Medical science has proven that the rib is one of the cells in a human body that can regrow itself and this explains why men and women have the same number of ribs.

More than six thousand years after God first performed the operation that created Eve, human beings are knocking at the door, attempting to create similar beings. With the biotechnological and medical advances of our day, human DNA can be extracted from a dead person, from the surface of a drinking glass, from cells deposited on a toothbrush, or even from a single hair stuck in a comb. Theoretically, this DNA could be inserted into a woman's egg to produce a human clone. Hence, there is no other method of "playing God" that makes the twenty-first century more like the days before the creation of woman and the days of Noah than the act of human cloning.

Ironically, although Eve was formed using Adam's DNA, it would be she and all women thereafter who would be responsible for the birthing of new human offspring because of their ability to produce the eggs needed for procreation to occur and to sustain the life of the embryo or fetus that develops in the uterus (womb). This is why the sons of God went after the daughters of men in their quest to procreate their kind. And for human cloning to occur today, the male DNA (or sperm) is not necessary.

Dolly the sheep was born without the sperm of a father because DNA from one ewe and another ewe's egg were all that was required. Dolly was cloned using three mothers: one provided the DNA (from the mammary glands), another the egg into which the DNA was inserted, and a third provided the womb that carried the embryo to full term.

UNDERSTANDING THE VARIOUS FORMS OF CLONING

COSEPUP defines human cloning as "… an assisted reproductive technology that would be carried out with the goal of creating a human being."[2] However, the technology or procedure that will enable scientists to create a human being is the same procedure used to create stem cells that could be used to cure diseases or to heal injuries. Differentiating between the two applications is where the rubber meets the road, resulting in ethical, religious, societal, scientific, and medical conundrum. Currently, there are two key aspects of the cloning enterprise that will affect our lives and our world in the foreseeable future: human reproductive cloning and nonreproductive cloning.

Human Reproductive Cloning

According to COSEPUP, reproductive cloning is the "... deliberate production of genetically identical individuals. Each newly produced individual is a clone of the original. Monozygotic (identical) twins are natural clones. Clones contain identical sets of genetic material in the nucleus—the compartment that contains the chromosomes—of every cell in their bodies. Thus, cells from two clones have the same DNA and the same genes in their nuclei."[3]

Two methods are commonly used for reproductive cloning, and they both require the implantation of an embryo (fertilized egg) into a uterus: embryonic stem cell cloning and cloning by embryo splitting.

Cloning by embryo splitting is a procedure that most people are familiar with because it is the basis for in vitro fertilization (IVF). This procedure unites the sperm and egg outside of a woman's body to produce a zygote or embryo. Since the DNA in embryo splitting is composed of the father's sperm and the mother's egg, it is similar to those formed naturally through sexual intercourse.

In animal embryonic cloning, adult DNA is inserted into a virgin female egg that has been stripped of all its own genetic material. The outcome is that the egg reprograms the adult cell (turns the 1's and 0's on or off), resulting in a cloned animal embryo that, when implanted in the uterus of a female animal, has the potential to grow into a genetic copy of the animal the DNA was taken from. This procedure is also known as cloning using somatic cell nuclear transfer (SCNT).

In order to create a successful animal (or human) clone, a large number of embryonic clones that show signs of deformity or result in miscarriages must be destroyed. These deformities are a result of bad reprogramming when the right 1's and 0's are turned on and off in the wrong places. It's like your computer monitor displaying only the typed phrase "beauty and the beast" when you were expecting to watch the movie.

In an ABCNEWS.COM article about Stem Cell cloning,[4] Amanda Onion noted that "…nearly 98 percent of attempts to clone animals have failed and those that do survive often appear abnormal and grossly enlarged." Since Dolly's cloning, animal cloning is progressively moving from one species to another. Scientists have already succeeded in cloning seven species of living creatures (sheep, mice, cows, pigs, goats, mule, and horses) with mostly horrible and abnormal results:

❑ Just to clone Dolly, scientists had to make about 272 attempts, and of those only Dolly made it to birth alive. Many of the attempts resulted in miscarriages and excessive deformities, while others grew beyond the normal fetus size and had to be terminated.

❑ Mules are a hybrid of a horse and a donkey. Mules are generally sterile and rarely are able to genetically reproduce themselves. To clone a mule, researchers at the University of Idaho and Utah State University extracted cells from developing mule fetuses. Then they harvested fertile eggs from mares and removed any genetic material from them. The researchers then surgically inserted the fetuses and the reconstructed eggs into the wombs of female horses. Out of the more than 300 embryos so implanted, only three developed into advanced embryos, leading to the birth of the first mule named Idaho Gem.

❑ To clone a horse, Italian researchers harvested eggs from dead adult female horses at a slaughterhouse and then cultured the eggs, removing any genetic material from them. The reconstructed eggs were placed next to the DNA that was taken from either a female or male horse skin cell and fused together by a burst of electricity. Out of the 841 embryos, 22 developed into advanced embryos, and seventeen of them were implanted into the nine mares. Four of the embryos advanced forward and only one made it to birth. The one that made it was named Prometea, after the Greek mythical character—Prometheus—who stole fire from the gods and gave it to humans.

Regardless of methodology or of animal species cloned, the ultimate goal of these preliminary breakthroughs is the cloning of humans. Many leading scientists, including Ian Wilmut, the British embryologist who led the team that cloned Dolly, do not support human cloning at this time because of the enormous risk of deformities and miscarriages and because of the burden that human society at large would have to bear should these creatures become part of our human population.

Even when human embryonic cloning could be successfully performed, scientists have already had visible evidence that cloned animals are not normal. Dolly was very fat and developed many adult ailments, including severe arthritis and lung disease, before she reached the age of five. "Cloned mice have developed into extremely overweight animals, cloned cows have been born with abnormally large hearts and lungs,"[5] and only God knows what cloned humans would look like. Perhaps, giant humans like the Nephilim!

After much dialogue on the pros and cons of human reproductive cloning, COSEPUP concluded that: "Data on the reproductive cloning of animals through the use of nuclear transplantation technology demonstrate that only a small percentage of attempts are successful; that many of the clones die during gestation, even in late stages; that newborn clones are often abnormal or die; and that the procedures may carry serious risks for the mother."[6]

Eventually though, human reproductive cloning will become a reality. Here are some of the potential drivers that COSEPUP identified[7]:

- ❏ Infertile couples who wish to have a child that is genetically identical with one of them, or with another nucleus donor
- ❏ Other individuals who wish to have a child that is genetically identical with them, or with another nucleus donor
- ❏ Parents who have lost a child and wish to have another, genetically identical child
- ❏ People who need a transplant (for example, of cord blood) to treat their own or their child's disease and who therefore wish to collect genetically identical tissue from a cloned fetus or newborn.

Another reason why human cloning may become popular in this century is that it might give same sex couples the opportunity to clone themselves, thus increasing their posterity outside of God's sovereign boundaries for the procreation of humanity.

In an article entitled "Can Men Make Eggs," Time Magazine reported:

> The debate about the use of embryonic stem cells to grow replacement tissue (brain, liver, etc.) is about to get much more complex now that scientists have turned stem cells from mouse embryos into viable eggs. The report in Science set researchers' imaginations ablaze. Could this technique provide an endless supply of human eggs? And since scientists turned cells from both female and male mice into eggs, could it overturn traditional notions of parenthood? Could males make egg cells? Could gay couples produce genetic offspring? So far, the research holds promise only for gay mice.[8]

Nonreproductive Cloning

Another popular application for embryonic cloning is what is termed nonreproductive cloning (also known as therapeutic cloning or research cloning). The same procedure used to create embryonic stem cells (ES) in reproductive cloning is also used for nonreproductive cloning. The difference is that the embryo is not implanted in a uterus and according to some scientists no live born clone is produced.

Therapeutic cloning would allow "the therapeutic benefits [to be] bestowed upon patients in need of treatments developed from a cloned embryo's stem cells."[9] For instance, patients suffering from severe facial burns could have cells removed from their body and inserted into a female egg. If an embryonic clone developed, the stem cells from the cloned embryo could be manipulated (the chemical formulation changed) to become skin cells that would be genetically identical to the patient's original skin cells. Once these new skin cells were transplanted into the patient's face, he or she would be able to recover nicely. However, the same embryo that produced the skin cell would normally proceed to become a human fetus and, eventually, a human baby, if implanted in a uterus. To prevent this from happening, the embryo would be destroyed as soon as its therapeutic value was extracted. According to Donal O'Mathuna:

> By definition, research on embryonic stem cells involves the destruction of some human beings for the so-called benefit of others. Therapeutic cloning goes one step further and entails the deliberate creation—as well the sacrifice—of human embryos for the alleged good of others. It treats human as a commodity to be manufactured when

needed and destroyed when desired to achieve some "greater" purpose. The utilitarian ethic, which justifies treating some humans as means to the end of benefiting others....are violations of human dignity.[10]

Because of the ethical issues involved in the destruction of a live cloned embryo, many are pushing for another type of cloning—the non-embryonic version. While this new form of cloning is still in its infancy, it attempts to create a non-cloned embryo that does not have human DNA. The problem with this version of cloning for therapeutic use is that cells from the embryo thus developed stand the chance of being rejected by the body of the patient receiving the transplant.

A more fundamental human and spiritual problem will arise when scientists succeed in cloning a human being through non-embryonic means. Should this become a reality, we would have a new human species that is not genetically related to Noah and his wife and thus, not descended from Adam and Eve.

Notes:

1. Genesis 2:23 (AMP).
2. Committee on Science, Engineering, and Public Policy, and Board on Life Sciences. 2002. Scientific and Medical Aspects of Human Cloning. National Academy Press.
3. Ibid, p. 24.
4. Amanda Onion, Hidden Flaws, Mouse Study Reveal Clones Appear Normal But Are Not, ABCNEWS.COM, August 6, 2001. Available at: http://abcnews.go.com/sections/scitech/DailyNews/cloningflaw010705.html.
5. Amanda Onion, op. cit.
6. Committee on Science, Engineering, and Public Policy, and Board on Life Sciences. 2002. Scientific and Medical Aspects of Human Cloning. National Academy Press, p. 93.
7. Ibid, p. 27.
8. Health Briefs. Can Men Make Eggs. Time Magazine, May 12, 2003, Vol. 161, No.19, page 84.
9. Donal O'Mathuna, Cloning and Stem Cell Research. Available at: http://www.cbhd.org/newsletter/002/002omathuna.htm
10. Ibid.

Chapter 6

THE ROLE OF GOD'S SPIRIT
IN HUMAN CONCEPTION

Two thousand years ago, the Holy Spirit implanted God's DNA into Mary's womb, making her pregnancy the "Immaculate Conception," and making Jesus, the Incarnate Son of God. Since the virgin conception of Jesus, many have doubted the feasibility of human conception without the contribution of a man's sperm. However, if mortal mankind could figure out how to clone a human being, why would the God of Creation not be able to implant His own DNA into a virgin and have her carry His Son from conception to birth?

One fundamental problem with the genetic engineering of humans that science can never solve is how to add God's Spirit into the conception and birth of a human being. The Creator God is the one "... who threw the skies into space, set earth on a firm foundation, and breathed his own life into men and women."[1] Although God delegated the responsibility for procreation to mankind (and to all animals), He still supervises the conception of every human being, because each human being is a reflection of His image and likeness.

Scientists have discovered that in the use of sperm and eggs for the conception of a child, the embryo or fetus that results has an imprint or mark of the DNA of both the father and the mother. Humans are known to have as many as 100 imprinted genes, and any number of these in a reproductively cloned human may cause problems or defects. However, from a spiritual dimension, at conception, when the embryo is formed, every

Figure 6-1

human fetus is always powered by God's Spirit. Psalm 104:30 captures this phenomenon accurately: "When you send your Spirit, they are created, and you renew the face of the earth." This is God's unchanging and universal role in the procreation of mankind, and it demonstrates His commitment and faithfulness to the human race. The Spirit of God in every person is where the purpose and meaning of life is imprinted, and science can never decode this mystery.

God's Spirit in mankind is the reason why every human being, no matter how demonically possessed their parents or creators might be, is born with dignity and into the appropriate generation, in order to reveal God's glory, as embedded in their life's pursuits, to the world. In spite of the fact that the sons of God and the daughters of men had children (contributing body and soul to their offspring), God was the only one who could have added His Spirit nature to every child conceived in these unions, to make each human offspring three-persons-in-one and an eternal being. In short, only God can start the heartbeat of every living creature, including human beings, even those whose lives begin in a petri dish.

To accept the fact that there are certain human beings who are conceived without a "spirit" or purpose in life would be to deny the role of God in every person's life. The Spirit of God is beyond man's ability to codify or to insert into the cloning process. When mankind begins to produce another breed of humanity from stripped genetic material, one has to wonder if God would keep inserting His Spirit into "petri dish" creations that are so devoid of His purpose for creating mankind in the first place.

The potential for human cloning in the twenty-first century has not only proven the feasibility of the virgin conception, it has also validated the concept

Figure 6-2

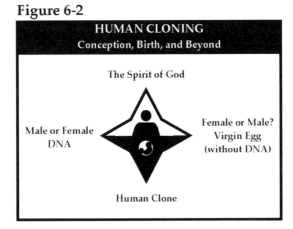

HUMAN CLONING
Conception, Birth, and Beyond

The Spirit of God

Male or Female
DNA

Female or Male?
Virgin Egg
(without DNA)

Human Clone

that a woman's "virgin" egg (without DNA material) can be fertilized by using adult DNA instead of a male sperm. At the rate of biotechnological and medical advances, it won't be long before genetically engineered DNA is used to fertilize a human egg. If the embryo from this experimentation grows to birth and beyond, we would have a half-human being that does not have as its base, the full genetic code of Noah. What such a being would look like, only God knows, but we can speculate that the term "monster" would not be an inappropriate description.

The ABCNEWS.COM article, cited earlier, continued: "… while clones showed no clear flaws in their genetic make-up, the animals did reveal problems in expressing their seemingly normal genes." What surprised the scientists was that some stem cells eventually survive to birth and beyond, and even if these clones appeared to be normal, they are not. In the same article, Mark Westhusin, a cloning expert at Texas A&M University in College Station, Texas, was quoted as saying that the "problems with genetic expression—the way information in genes is manifested in the body—are difficult to detect and this makes the practice of cloning even more dangerous...it's not gene mutation, it's gene expression...this is not something you can set up a test to prevent."

A more fundamental issue with human cloning, both in Noah's day (when God declared that His Spirit would not contend with man forever) and in our own day, is the issue of personal accountability. Just as Cain was responsible to God for the murder of Abel, every human being is accountable to God for their actions while they are on earth. However, when a person has cloned an exact replica of himself or herself, who then is responsible for the actions of the clone? When Lamech and the other sons of God chose to clone themselves, they theoretically kept themselves humanly alive beyond the seventh generation that God had limited Cain's line to, even though they were no longer present in human bodies.

Impact of Generational Blessings and Curses on Clones

While parents, society, and life experiences play a major role in a person's lifestyle, there is still something to be said for gene expression, a product of imprinting of the donor's DNA mark on the embryo. According to COSEPUP,

> *Imprinted genes usually have a "mark" imposed on or near them in the egg or the sperm, so the copy of a gene inherited from the mother behaves differently from the copy inherited from the father....For normal development to occur, an embryo needs one set of chromosomes with the imprints imposed by the father and another set with imprints imposed by the mother.*[2]

In the spiritual dimension, imprinted genes may very well be where generational blessings and curses are registered leading to inherited gene expressions. Remember that God put a mark on Cain as part of his judgment. While this mark may have been a physical one, it is probable that it became a genetic imprinting in subsequent generations of the sons of God. This genetic imprinting limited their abilities to procreate their kind in sufficient numbers and slated their extinction by the seventh generation.

Genetic imprinting errors have been associated with fetal abnormalities and death, leading COSEPUP to conclude that: "In humans, mutations that perturb or inactivate one copy of an imprinted region can result in the development of tumors in children or adults or several well-known genetic disorders in children."[3]

This may help explain why the Nephilim were such abnormal human beings because they carried the imprints of the "cursed" sons of God and the "blessed" daughters of men. Just as the Nephilim could not resolve their "in-flight debacle," neither can we adequately rule out the impact of DNA in a clone's psychosocial behavior. We certainly cannot mitigate against generational curses and blessings by manipulating chemical formulations.

Admittedly, DNA is not the only determinant of a person's behavior, and while clones may be genetically identical, their physical and behavioral characteristics may not be identical. However, if we can use DNA today to convict a person of a crime, it won't be long before we use the same DNA to explain why he or she committed that crime. When human cloning becomes a reality, one of the fundamental questions court systems across the globe will have to grapple with is determining responsibility for crimes committed by a person who also has multiple identical copies of himself or herself. This is why God, in His infinite wisdom, made each person unique.

Is the clone(s) responsible for the crime of its parent or vice versa? Remember, a clone is not just an offspring, but an identical genetic copy of the adult who produced it. When Lamech killed a young man for wounding him, he subjected all of his Nephilim children to the same generational curse of extinction that had plagued the lineage of Cain.

Would the clones of a serial killer who has cloned himself or herself and blames his or her defective DNA for the crimes be sentenced to death along with the killer? Extend these scenarios to the possible millions of cloned fetuses that might have survived to birth and beyond during Noah's day, and you begin to see God's wisdom in destroying the entire world by flood and beginning again with Noah and his descendants to reestablish on earth a new human species that we are a part of today.

FIGURE 6-3
HUMAN REPRODUCTIVE CLONING

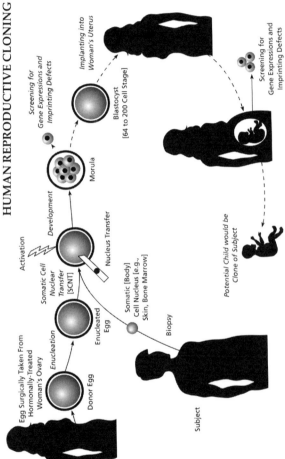

Reprinted with permission from Scientific and Medical Aspects of Human Reproductive Cloning (2002) by the The National Academy of Sciences, courtesy of the National Academies Press, Washington D.C. Original Image Enhanced by Jack Lowry of Jack Lowry Design, Danville, California

FIGURE 6-4
HUMAN NONREPRODUCTIVE CLONING (Nuclear Transplantation to Produce Stem Cells)

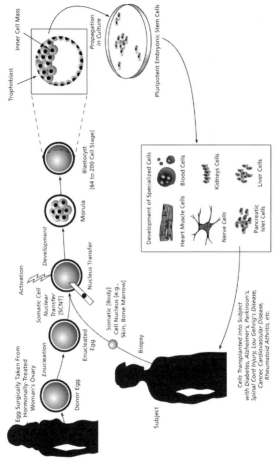

Reprinted with permission from Scientific and Medical Aspects of Human
Reproductive Cloning (2002) by the The National Academy of Sciences,
courtesy of the National Academies Press, Washington D.C. Original Image
Enhanced by Jack Lowry of Jack Lowry Design, Danville, California.

Notes:

1. Zechariah 12:1 (MSG).
2. Committee on Science, Engineering, and Public Policy, and Board on Life Sciences. 2002. Scientific and Medical Aspects of Human Cloning. National Academy Press., p. 44.
3. Ibid, p. 44.

Chapter 7

COMPARING NOAH'S WORLD
TO OUR WORLD

Understanding the theological implication for why fallen angels could not have been the fathers to the Nephilim is key in acknowledging the sovereignty of God over all of life. A Holy and righteous God who came down to form mankind (without the assistance of Satan) would not have allowed such external infiltration or distortion of His purpose. Human beings possessed by demons are not the same as angelic-human offspring. Only human beings, because of our godlike procreation capabilities, can change the gene pool of humanity by cloning. Making this differentiation allows us to see why our generation is so very much like Noah's generation. Jesus said in Matthew 24:37 that *"As it was in the days of Noah, so it will be at the coming of the*

Son of Man."

Since Jesus equated the events leading to Noah's flood with the events surrounding His Second Coming, His comparison of the two God world orders provides the foundation for our understanding the Nephilim world and comparing that world to today's world. To ensure that we are not comparing apples to oranges, we will look at the structures or principles (creativity, drive, possibilities, and achievements) in the two worlds as opposed to the forms of existence (type of food, clothing, hair style) in those worlds.

Two distinguishing characteristics of the Nephilim were that they were "heroes of old" (because of their heritage as sons of God) and "men of renown" (because of their knowledge of the world and because of their inventions). They seemed to have defied God's curse and established their lifespan and civilization forever. In like manner, our human origin goes back to Seth, and our heritage to Noah and his family.

In the beginning, the immortal human sons of God born of spirit were able to move about the earth and heavens freely. Never since has there been a generation of mankind that has crisscrossed the length and breadth of the earth more than our current generation. To achieve this capability, mankind studied birds for thousands of years—awed by their abilities to soar above gravitational forces—and in the twentieth century developed machines to mimic what birds do naturally. While the original sons of God were able to travel vast distances because they were not subject to electromagnetic and gravitational forces the way we are, we have been able to invent traveling devices like parachutes, balloons, airplanes, rockets, shuttles, etc. In the twentieth century, our generation has been able to send men into space and to the moon and discover new planets and galaxies. Someday soon we may make traveling to space for summer vacations en vogue.

If we were to list some of the "supernatural" things that we can do today because of the inventions of our minds and compare them to what the sons of God did by virtue of their godlike nature, there would be more similarities now than during any other time of human history since the flood. Furthermore, if it were possible to poll the people from all of the generations of humanity that have lived since the time of the flood and ask them to describe our generation, the one term that would probably surface would be "heroes anew," just as the sons of God were called "heroes of old."

All of our acquired knowledge is helping us understand the human body more than any generation since the flood. Our knowledge of how the human body is put together has been developed from many different fields—from engineering to metaphysics. For example, advances in medicine could only go so far until technological innovations caught up. The fusion of biotechnology and medicine has allowed our generation to be able to look at human cloning as a possibility for the first time since Lamech pioneered it with the Nephilim.

While the sons of God and the daughters of men achieved their own version of human cloning by sexual intercourse, we will soon achieve our own version in the laboratory. Again, if we were to poll all the generations of humanity since the flood, our achievements in the late twentieth- and early twenty-first century would earn us the title, "men and women of renown."

We will now continue our comparison of cloning in Noah's time and our own with three unique God-centered perspectives: God's end-time messages and assignments, human responses to God's end-time purposes, and God's desired outcome versus the actual and potential results.

GOD'S END-TIME MESSAGES AND ASSIGNMENTS

One of the distinguishing characteristics of Seth's lineage—the sons of men—was that it was during their generation that "… men began to call on [or proclaim] the name of the LORD."[1] On the other hand, the sons of God did not have much use for a God who had sentenced their lineage to extinction.

Proclaiming the relevance, grace, mercy, and authority of God in all of life was the good news message that the sons of men were commissioned to disseminate to their world. Although it appeared that Lamech, the sixth generation of the sons of God, had succeeded in breaking the curse on his lineage, Enoch, in the sixth generation of the sons of men, knew that God's judgment could not be overturned by human willpower and creativity.

The Spirit of God authored the message of
righteousness   that   Enoch   was   divinely
commissioned to preach to his contemporaries.
Enoch understood the times and knew that Lamech's
"final solution" to the extinction decree by means of
human cloning would not stand. Because Enoch took
God's message seriously, he may also have received
foreknowledge about God's timeline for the end of
his age. He suggested this foreknowledge when he
named his first son, Methuselah, which means: "the
flood shall come when he dies."[2]

God also took notice of Enoch's decision to
steadfastly proclaim the good news of righteousness.
As a result, Enoch was translated into the afterlife
without experiencing physical death. Ironically, the
eternal life Lamech sought by disobedience and
defiance, God easily granted to Enoch for seeking to
do right. In addition, God allowed Enoch's son
Methuselah to outlive most of the human clones. God
assigned Methuselah's grandson, Noah, the task of
sounding the last call message of God's grace and
mercy.

In like manner, Jesus, the Incarnate Son of God,
came to proclaim the good news of God's provision
of redemption for all of mankind. At the time, He

unashamedly declared: "I am the way and the truth and the life. No one comes to the Father except through me."[3] Just before He ascended into heaven, Jesus commissioned His disciples in every generation to continue the divine assignment, saying

> *All authority in heaven and on earth has been given to me. Therefore go and make disciples of all nations, baptizing them in the name of the Father and of the Son and of the Holy Spirit, and teaching them to obey everything I have commanded you. And surely I am with you always, to the very end of the age.*[4]

The good news of humanity's redemption is a living message that every Christian through his or her everyday life is supposed to proclaim to the world. And through our everyday choices, the message that the "… wages of sin is death, but the gift of God is eternal life in [or through] Christ Jesus our Lord,"[5] ought to be so clear in its power to transform evil into good that it attracts people to receive the free gift of salvation for themselves.

HUMAN RESPONSES
TO GOD'S END-TIME PURPOSES

The seed of rebellion

Seeking eternal life here on earth is the common goal shared by the sons of God and those seeking human cloning in our world today. While scientists in the late twentieth- and early twenty-first-century may boast of the possibility of human cloning as a new frontier in the ever-increasing human knowledge base, the first human experimentation with cloning actually occurred more than five thousand years ago, when the sons of God and the daughters of men produced a new type of human being— a hybrid sons-of-God-sons-of-men species.

Despite being a blend of supernatural and natural humanity, the Nephilim were still referred to as the "sons of God" because their sons of God heredity was dominant. In other words, the Nephilim that survived through conception, birth, and beyond were identical to Lamech or whichever other son of God had provided the sperm (DNA) from which they had been cloned. Although the original sons of God were no longer living in flesh and blood, they were still alive through their Nephilim clones—for what their progenitors thought would be forever.

The sons of God only wanted to remove the curse of extinction from their lineage, but in the twenty-first century human cloning offers many medical and cosmetic benefits. Nevertheless, the net result is the same: using some human beings for the benefits of others. As a result of stem cell research, this generation and future generations of mankind are once again likely to welcome genetically identical human clones into the world.

In addition, people of many sects who have no use for an almighty God would make human cloning their chosen method of securing eternal life on earth. One might continue to make copies of himself or herself in sufficient quantities to live forever. At least, that is the claim. In the fall of 2002, a "sect with peculiar opinion" (about being from Mars) shocked the world by announcing that they had cloned the first human being. While we may never know if they succeeded or not, the fact is that sooner or later human cloning will become a reality. According to this sect, the Raelians, their "… goal is to give humans eternal life through cloning."

The wholesale rejection of
God's purpose for His world

Noah's generation was notorious for abandoning God's purpose for His world and for living out their lives according to fleshly (body and soul) dictate. Once the sons of God were able to produce their kind, the role of God in determining man's everyday existence became superfluous. The existence of the Nephilim was, by far, the most devastating reason for God's irrelevance. If the Cainites could have gotten away with their disobedience to God, there would be no reason for this generation to take Noah's message seriously.

However, the Nephilim would never have existed if the sons of men had taken their divine assignment seriously. The bottom line is that the godly sons of men failed in their assignment to convince the ungodly people in their generation to return to the restoration plan that had been given by God to mankind. As a result, they too were caught committing the same ungodly acts for which the sons of God were famous. Sadly, the year that Methuselah died, these generations of the two human species were so engrossed in their delusions that they missed the signs of the impending deluge.

When Jesus opened the way back to the Father, He expected those redeemed by His blood to transform the world by the power to demonstrate the good news message at work in their lives. Just as the people of Noah's time turned away from his message to live righteously, it seems as though two thousand years after Jesus established His church, the world is influencing the church more than the church is influencing the world in righteous living. From the arts to interpreting history, from everyday work strategies to philosophies of life, Christians are imitating the world instead of leading the way in establishing cultural norms, thereby fulfilling another end-time warning of Jesus: "At that time many will turn away from the faith and will betray and hate each other, and many false prophets will appear and deceive many people."[6]

Admittedly, there are many godly theologians and teachers who have written books about the Nephilim and have taught that they were the sons of fallen angels. There are denominations today that have based some of their doctrines on the belief in angelic-human hybrids. To convince some of these teachers to change their views is a daunting task, but the repercussions for holding on to their beliefs are far worse, when we consider the number of people who may end up in hell. Interestingly, while Jesus' comparison of Noah's world before the flood and our world has proven accurate in many ways, we are yet to see giant, angelic-human offspring roaming the earth. Yet, soon we may see an assortment of giant human clones roaming our earth.

The escalation of wickedness in the world

The Bible never talked about the population of the Nephilim, partly because their numbers were insignificant when compared to the booming population of the sons of men. What is significant, though, is that the practice of cloning in Noah's time had gotten so out of hand that all kinds of unnatural creatures were being formed. The Nephilim as a species were said to be giants and were known as the "fallen ones," because of their genetic adulteration and their inability to move between the natural and supernatural realms with their hybrid bodies.

By way of comparison, most of the animals that scientists have succeeded in cloning in the twenty-first century have been giant-sized creatures much larger than their original genetic source, confirming the biblical account of what happens when you mix two different gene pools together. According to COSEPUP, animal cloning,

> [R]esults in a wide variety of abnormalities, including greater than normal size (both during gestation and after birth), greater early- and late-gestation fetal morbidity and mortality, greater postnatal mortality, and various developmental defects in the immune, cardiovascular, and possibly nervous systems. (Subtle behavioral and mental defects might be undetectable in animal models.) In addition to the risks inherent in the overproduction of oocytes from egg donors, increased maternal morbidity and mortality are to be expected.[7]

The unnatural process of animal cloning and the life of Dolly the sheep provide us a glimpse of what to expect with human cloning and also points to the consequences of the rush to create human sons of God clones in Noah's time. If 98% of all attempts to clone animals fail, imagine how many daughters of men groaned in pain and paid with their lives to carry giant fetuses in wombs that had not been made for such creatures. Remember, Eve had a problem carrying Cain in her womb, and when he was delivered she exclaimed that she had "… acquired a man from the LORD." If the first lady of humanity suffered to carry the fetuses of the sons of God, and if she was equipped for the task (and assisted by God Himself), imagine just how many daughters of men died in the process of carrying the Nephilim and how many Nephilim did not survive to full term birth from all the attempts?

While we may never know the number of clones that existed during Noah's day, we do know from our experiences now with animal cloning that many human lives must have been lost to produce them. Judging from the high percentage of miscarriages and deformities in animal cloning today and, potentially, from human cloning in the future, it is also possible that not all unions between the sons of God and the daughters of men yielded Nephilim clones. This may be one of the reasons why there seemed to have been a mad rush by the sons of God to marry the daughters of men, not only because they were "beautiful to behold," but probably because they provided the eggs needed for procreation to occur and many of the women were dying carrying the Nephilim fetus. Again, medical science may have shed the light on this phenomenon. In its findings, COSEPUP acknowledged that although some organization may attempt to clone a human:

> [S]uch attempts would most likely fail [because] there is a high probability they would be associated with serious risks to any possible fetus or newly born child and may harm the woman carrying the developing fetus....In addition, because of the large number of eggs needed for such experiments, many more women would be exposed to the risks inherent in egg donation for a single cloning attempt than for the reproduction of a child by the presently used in vitro fertilization (IVF) techniques. These medical and scientific findings lead us to conclude that the procedures are now unsafe for humans.[8]

When wickedness gets out of control

When the sons of men who had been entrusted with the good news failed to proclaim it to their next of kin and to the sons of God clones, wickedness became widespread. It is possible that the Nephilim sons of God not only cloned themselves, but also cloned their livestock and other living creatures in their sphere of influence, as they were also subject to Cain's curse. Our generation of humanity, like

Noah's generation, has also cloned a variety of animals on our way to create a human clone. Remember that it was one of the Nephilim sons of Lamech who introduced the livestock-shepherding trade.

This may also explain why the only living creatures that made it into the ark were those God Himself handpicked and sent to Noah: "Two of every kind of bird, of every kind of animal and of every kind of creature that moves along the ground will come to you to be kept alive."[9] The point is that Noah's generation had gotten so decadent that their souls (feelings) governed their bodies at the expense of the Spirit of God, leading God to declare in Genesis 6:5-7:

> *The LORD saw how great man's wickedness on the earth had become, and that every inclination of the thoughts of his heart was only evil all the time. The LORD was grieved that he had made man on the earth, and his heart was filled with pain. So the LORD said, I will wipe mankind, whom I have created, from the face of the earth — men and animals, and creatures that move along the ground, and birds of the air—for I am grieved that I have made them.*

We don't have to see billions of human clones to know that we are approaching the time of the end of our age. Never, since the time of Noah has the community of mankind seen such a proliferation of sexual perversity, degradation of family values, and complacency toward God's role and purpose for His world. Our generation has taken fleshly pursuits (wickedness) to a level of decadence equal only to that of Noah's generation. The Apostle Paul described wickedness as follows:

> Now the doings (practices) of the flesh are clear (obvious): they are immorality, impurity, indecency, idolatry, sorcery, enmity, strife, jealousy, anger (ill temper), selfishness, divisions (dissensions), party spirit (factions, sects with peculiar opinions, heresies), envy, drunkenness, carousing, and the like. I warn you beforehand, just as I did previously, that those who do such things shall not inherit the kingdom of God.[10]

Today, sexual perversity has reached such proportions that, thanks to the Internet, it is possible for millions of people around the world to be bound in the same sexual experiences, all at once. Today, children can be conceived not only outside of a marriage relationship, but also outside of a mother's womb—with or without a male sperm. They can be conceived without the gene material in an egg (stem cell cloning), and for many other reasons besides procreation. While a man would still need a woman's egg in order to clone himself, a woman could contribute her own egg and DNA to produce a clone of herself. Furthermore, there is no telling what varieties of human clones we will see roaming the earth in the end time.

It would also be possible to obtain a man's DNA from his hairbrush, insert it into an egg, and manipulate it to produce a female version of that man. What would stop a demon-possessed person from inserting a dead man's DNA into an egg and producing a living human offspring for the dead? What about those who might want to defy God by inserting human DNA into a fish egg, producing the Little Mermaid in real life, not just a mythical story?

When children cloned from stem cells become a reality, do we treat these as humans like ourselves, or as strange creatures? The science behind cloning will only get better, and someday we might just be able to create a perfect simulation of a mother's womb in the laboratory. Imagine a scientist manipulating the cells in an embryo in order to produce new cells to cure a person's abnormal eyelid, only to have the embryo develop first into a fetus and then into a living being with a giant head, giant lungs, irregular heartbeat, and no other definable body parts. Is this creature a human being or a monster? Monstrous as it may be, as long as this creature is breathing, the Spirit of God is living in it.

Unless it was revealed to them by God, there is no way that the early church fathers could have known that cloned animals are often giant replicas of their DNA parent and are often abnormal or unnatural. Yet, this is how they described the Nephilim. God has the final say in how much He will allow mankind, with all our biotechnological and medical advances, to change the genetic makeup of humans as He created them in His image and likeness.

GOD'S DESIRED OUTCOME VERSUS ACTUAL AND POTENTIAL RESULTS

God's desired outcome

When Noah's generation drowned out the Spirit of God from their everyday lives and continued to ignore His declared purpose for His world, it lost its purpose and the meaning of life, prompting God to declare: "My Spirit will not contend with man forever, for he is mortal; his days will be a hundred and twenty years."[11] God set the timeframe of one hundred and twenty years in order to give Noah time to proclaim the gospel of righteousness to his generation—a message they wholeheartedly rejected. While Methuselah's long life served as the signpost for God's grace period for mankind in that era, Noah's ark was a provision of mercy for those who wanted to repent and thus escape the imminent demise of the world.

If we believe that the Nephilim were offspring of fallen angels who overpowered the daughters of men and transformed their culture into a wicked and godless one, then it would be very easy for us either to become demoralized and throw our hands in the air over the same depravity that we see in our world today or to become selective about which group of people we would invest our time and money in trying to reach with the good news message. However, Jesus is both the Son of God and the Son of Man, and God's criteria for the redemption of human beings through Him was revealed in John 3:16-18:

> *For God so loved the world that he gave his one and only Son, that whoever believes in him shall not perish but have eternal life. For God did not send his Son into the world to condemn the world, but to save the world through him. Whoever believes in him is not condemned, but whoever does not believe stands condemned already because he has not believed in the name of God's one and only Son.*

When Jesus compared Noah's world before the flood to our current world, He wanted to motivate both those whose spirits have already been redeemed by His blood to go to all the nations and make disciples and those who had yet to respond positively to His good news message to do so while there was still time.

While the advent of human cloning in our generation puts us in our own end time world, it does not give us the authority to set dates about the Second Coming of Jesus. Speaking in Matthew 24:36-39, Jesus forewarned,

> *No one knows about that day or hour, not even the angels in heaven, nor the Son, but only the Father. As it was in the days of Noah, so it will be at the coming of the Son of Man. For in the days before the flood, people were eating and drinking, marrying and giving in marriage, up to the day Noah entered the ark; and they knew nothing about what would happen until the flood came and took them all away. That is how it will be at the coming of the Son of Man.*

The "people" in the days of Noah who Jesus was referring to were human beings—both those with the DNA of the sons of God and those with the DNA of the sons of men. And Jesus compared them to our present generation. After waiting for Jesus' eminent return for over two thousand years, many have given up hope that He will ever come back as He promised.

God's intended outcome for the 120 years He assigned Noah to preach righteousness was that none of the world's people would drown from the impending deluge. God wanted them to heed Noah's warning and be saved. His intentions today are still the same—that none should perish. By tying the timeline for the impending deluge to Methuselah's lifespan, God hoped to make it so obvious that no one with this information would be caught by surprise. However, the people in Noah's day paid no attention the year that Methuselah died and concentrated instead on ridiculing Noah for his unusual ark construction project.

In like manner, instead of paying attention to the sign of the reappearance of Nephilim-type creatures in our end time, some continue to preach that fallen angels were the fathers of the Nephilim, while the rest of the world ridicules such a concept and thus ignores this obvious sign of the Second Coming of the Son of God.

God's actual
results in Noah's day

Sadly, only eight people responded to God's invitation and made it into the ark—Noah, his three sons, and their wives—out of the millions and possibly billions of souls.

God's potential
results in our day

Just as Noah and his family entered the ark and the remainder of the whole world was destroyed by flood, so can we be certain of the Second Coming of Jesus when the gospel is preached to the whole world. Jesus said in Matthew 24:30-31 that,

> *At that time the sign of the Son of Man will appear in the sky, and all the nations of the earth will mourn. They will see the Son of Man coming on the clouds of the sky, with power and great glory. And he will send his angels with a loud trumpet call, and they will gather his elect from the four winds, from one end of the heavens to the other.*

The bottom line for our generation is that if Jesus is correct when He says He is the "only way" back to God, then four billion or more people in our world today will not go to heaven, compared to the two billion who profess to be Christians. This is in defiance of God's heart cry that He did not want any human being to end up in hell.

According to Harvard University Professor Samuel P. Huntington, "In the modern world religion is a central, perhaps the central, force tha motivates and mobilizes people....The Cold War division of humanity is over. The more fundamental divisions of humanity in terms of ethnicity, religion, and civilization remain and spawn new conflicts."[12]

From a humanistic point of view, Huntington concluded:

> *In the long run, however, Mohammed wins out. Christianity spreads primarily by conversion, Islam by conversion and reproduction. The percentage of Christians in the world peaked at about 30 percent in the 1980s, leveled off, is now declining, and will probably approximate about 25 percent of the world's population by 2025.*[13]

According to the United Nations global population estimates, there will be about 8.3 billion people in the world by 2025. Using Huntington's percentage and Jesus' declaration about being the only way back to God, we can assume that 6.2 billion people will not spend eternity with God. If this statistical prediction comes true, then we will have become exactly like the world Noah preached to, with or without angelic-human beings roaming the earth and producing a different breed of humanity.

Notes:

1. Genesis 4:26.
2. Pink, Arthur W., Gleanings in Genesis, Moody Bible Institute, Chicago IL, 1922. Note: Arthur W. Pink in his book, Gleanings From Genesis, explains the meaning of Methuselah as implying "when he is dead, it shall be sent."
3. John 14:6.
4. Matthew 28:18-20.
5. Romans 6:23.
6. Matthew 24:10-14.
7. Committee on Science, Engineering, and Public Policy, and Board on Life Sciences. 2002. Scientific and Medical Aspects of Human Cloning. National Academy Press, p. 52.
8. Ibid, p. 95, 93.
9. Genesis 6:20.
10. Galatians 5:19-21 (AMP).
11. Genesis 6:3.
12. Huntington, Samuel P., The Clash of Civilizations and the Remaking of World Order, Touchstone, New York, NY, 1997, pg. 66-67.
13. Ibid, pg. 65-66.

Chapter 8

LIFE MATTERS AND
THE MYSTERY OF THE AFTERLIFE

Modern science has created a better life for modern humanity. Science has taught us much about ourselves—about our bodies in particular and about the universe in general. It is because of scientific discoveries that we can now decipher such concepts as the Immaculate Conception, which were once impossible to understand beyond acceptance on the basis of blind faith. We can now use DNA technology to solve ancient mysteries, and we can use our understanding of how the universe functions to send human beings into space. But, science has not been able to uncover the meaning of life or the reason why life on earth is short while eternity is forever. We need religion to add meaning to the knowledge and achievements of science.

IN THE AGE OF SCIENTIFIC DISCOVERIES, WHO NEEDS GOD?

What if you do not believe that there is a God who rules the affairs of humankind? Why should the re-emergence of human cloning be of concern to you? Who needs God when we can clone a human being, send humans to the moon, or use evolution to explain how mankind came into existence? The basic issue is eternal life. Every human being wants to live forever, either in this world or in the afterlife. This is why the anti-aging and the afterlife (both religious and pyschic) industries thrive even when other parts of the economy are doing badly. Whether people are living in the most deplorable conditions or in the most palatial environments, all would give up everything they had to buy extra time in this life or to obtain eternal life after death. However, no one can truthfully believe in an afterlife without first believing that there is a God.

Interestingly, one of the best scientific minds of the seventeenth century, Blaise Pascal, concluded that to believe that God does or does not exist is like gambling. Pascal, who was renowned for formulating the "Decision Theory" and the "Probability Theory" in mathematics, argued that the probability that God exists far outweighs the probability that He does not exist. This is what is known as Pascal's Wager.

Pascal contended that if you believe that God exists and you are right, then you're a winner. If you believe that God exists and He does not, then you have lost nothing. If you believe that God does not exists and He does not, then you have also lost nothing. However if you don't believe that God exists and He does, then you have lost—big time!

Figure 8-1

Pascal's Wager	God Exists	God Does Not Exist
If you believe that God exists	Winner	Lost Nothing
If you believe that God does not exists	Loser	Lost Nothing

In spite of our scientific accomplishments, no human being today is as naturally intelligent as Adam and Eve were. In our time, in order to become a credible expert, one must specialize in a certain field or fields, but Adam and Eve were experts in every human endeavor because their teacher and mentor was God. Adam and Eve had perfect knowledge about the origin of the universe and how it functioned, as well as about the composition of the human genome—a discovery that took modern mankind several millennia to understand. Adam named all the animal species in our world, including his wife—a feat that has never been repeated by mortal mankind—at least not on the same scale. Even if a person were born with half the knowledge that Adam and Eve had at their creation, he or she would still have less than one hundred and twenty years to use it before entering eternity.

No scientific inventions can make our world more conducive to life than the pristine earth Adam and Eve occupied after their banishment from the garden. Furthermore, every one of our scientific discoveries and achievements today is only an imperfect replica of the world of wonder and discoveries that Adam and Eve made and explored under the guidance of the Creator. Even our ability to send humans into space is only an imitation of the supernatural abilities that Adam and Eve and the sons of God enjoyed.

Just as God functions in three persons—Father, Son, and Holy Spirit—human beings are created to function as spirit, body, and soul. The body and soul together constitute true human nature (flesh), and they were not made to ever be separate from each other. Yet, because of Adam and Eve's sin, after a mortal lifetime of opportunities to make it right with God, the body and the soul are sentenced at death to be separated from each other temporarily. For the lineage of Cain, the judgment that Cain received hastened the permanent separation of their bodies and souls, making them wandering spirits on earth. Scripture teaches that at the end of time there will be a Second Judgment Day, when Satan and all wandering spirits and souls will be cast into a lake of fire in a second death sentence.[1] This is also known as eternal damnation—the opposite of eternal life in God's Presence.

DEAD ENDS IN THE
PURSUIT OF ETERNAL LIFE

On September 11, 2001, nineteen hijackers commandeered four airplanes, slamming three into buildings and crashing the fourth in the fields of Pennsylvania. Thousands of people were killed. The Al Queda operatives who were Muslims gave up their earthly lives in hopes of achieving eternity with God by destroying innocent lives and throwing countless families into an unnecessary lifetime of pain and suffering. What righteous God would allow such creatures into His Presence? After all, He banished Adam and Eve from that Presence merely because they had eaten the forbidden fruit.

Yet, after Adam and Eve's crime against humanity, God set in motion a process that would allow them to regain eternal life. Adam and Eve did nothing on their own behalf to earn eternal life in God's Presence once they had lost it. Instead, God came to them and made a sacrifice on their behalf that kept them from the sentence of instant death that their disobedience warranted.

Lamech realized that his offspring would be the last of the lineage of the sons of God in human flesh, so he sought to gain eternal life on earth by human cloning. However, Lamech's strategy backfired because his act of murder caused the quickening of the extinction of his human clones from the face of the earth through Noah's flood.

If Adam and Eve could not reason their way back into God's Presence after the fall, and if Lamech could not obtain eternal life on earth by human cloning, neither can modern man achieve eternal life outside of God's way. Because God so loved Adam and Eve, He banished them to a temporary lifetime on earth until they died physically and returned either to an eternal life in God's Presence or to an eternal damnation away from God. This was the first judgment. This same love that God had for the first human couple extends to all of their offspring in every generation, including you and me. To live eternally in God's Presence requires nothing from humankind other than acceptance of God's free gift. You do not have to kill people or maim yourself in the name of God or pay an intermediary to have your clone made in order to achieve eternal life. In fact, since A.D. 30, when Jesus was crucified, God's way to eternal life in His Presence does not have to cost you anything, period.

HOW TO OBTAIN ETERNAL LIFE IN GOD'S PRESENCE

One evening I was awakened by the sound of my phone ringing. The caller identified himself as a radio disc jockey and informed me that all I had to do to win a free ticket to a sold out concert that weekend was to say which station was the best radio station in town. I instantly gave the name of the station that I listen to regularly, and the disc jockey apologized and hung up. I had failed to say the name or the call letters of the station that the disc jockey represented, and so I failed to receive the free ticket. Receiving eternal life is as simple as declaring (confessing) the right station name or call letters that the Creator has designated, and accepting the terms of the offer.

Every human being faces the same choices that Adam and Eve faced when God confronted them for their disobedience. He sacrificed an animal and made garments of clothing for them. With all of their sophisticated knowledge of good and evil, Adam and Eve accepted God's sacrifice as a free gift and gladly wore the animal clothing God had made for them. As they set out to pursue God's purpose in His world, the clothing served as a covering for their sins. Their banishment redeemed the first couple from becoming wandering spirits on earth, while blocking their access to the tree of life that would have enabled them to live eternally in God's Presence even in their fallen state. If you had seen Adam and Eve in their new spiritual garments, they would have gladly confessed that they had obtained them by God's grace and mercy.

Two thousand years ago, God made a greater sacrifice when He allowed His Only Son to pay the permanent ultimate price for humankind's redemption. You do not have to join a church, belong to any religious order, or recite a particular creed in order to receive your own free ticket to eternal life. Since flesh gives birth to flesh and spirit to spirit, the Holy Spirit of God is the only one who can reveal this truth to your spirit and give you the option to choose between living eternally in God's Presence or becoming a wandering soul until the Second Judgment Day sends you to eternal damnation.

To receive eternal life today, all you have to do is believe with your heart and declare with your mouth that Jesus Christ is LORD. Your heart—not your head—is required for this initial step, because restoring fellowship with God begins where that fellowship was first broken—in the heart. The head is where humans process the acquired knowledge of good and evil—the aftermath of the broken heart-relationship with God. That is why you and I cannot use the knowledge of good and evil to know, to understand, or to be reconciled with God.

The simplicity of the truth is a major hurdle to obtaining eternal life

The notion that we can obtain eternal life so easily makes it difficult for some people to believe in it. That is why the idea of salvation by good works appeals to so many people. Compared to our awareness of our own sinful nature, God's free offer of salvation sounds too good to be true. However, when we stand before a righteous God, our good works are about as useful as wearing clothes made of fig leaves would be on a cold winter morning.

The ease of obtaining eternal life God's way is another reason human cloning seems, on the surface, to be the most plausible way to live forever. It is complicated and requires enormous intellectual capital, not to mention financial resources. But, the desire to live forever in a body that was not designed for eternity is an exercise in futility. Remember that in times past, the advent of human cloning caused God to set in motion another judgment that led to a massive global flood.

Therefore, accepting God's blood sacrifice, which covers over all of your sins, is the most intelligent choice to make—and best of all, it will cost you nothing! While the gift of salvation is free to us, it cost God His Only Son. In his classic book, 'My Utmost for His Highest,' Oswald Chambers wrote:

> *The agony in the Garden was the agony of the Son of God in fulfilling His destiny as the Savior of the world. The veil is pulled back here to reveal all that it cost Him to make it possible for us to become sons of God. His agony was the basis for the simplicity of our salvation. The Cross of Christ was a triumph for the Son of Man. It was not only a sign that our Lord had triumphed, but that He had triumphed to save the human race. Because of what the Son of Man went through, every human being can now get through into the very Presence of God.*

What if a person has
never heard of Jesus?

What if someone has never heard of Jesus, and dies, only to face Him on judgment day as LORD? The answer is simple. God is a righteous judge who cannot hold someone responsible for not knowing about the free gift of eternal life through Christ Jesus. According to Scripture, those who have never heard of Christ before or after His death will be judged by the "good and evil" standard. And what is "good"? Solomon articulated the truth of this when he wrote about what every human being knows innately:

> *All has been heard; the end of the matter is: Fear God [revere and worship Him, knowing that He is] and keep His commandments, for this is the whole of man [the full, original purpose of his creation, the object of God's providence, the root of character, the foundation of all happiness, the adjustment to all inharmonious circumstances and conditions under the sun] and the whole [duty] for every man. For God shall bring every work into judgment, with every secret thing, whether it is good or evil.*[2]

Every person in every culture knows the difference between good and evil—this is not a mystery to humanity. Every culture also has its own awareness and name for a higher power or God. As a righteous judge, when He passes judgment on one where there is no covering from His Son, God examines the intent of the heart. So, for those people who have never heard of Jesus, to earn a place in God's Presence forever, the weight of their good works must be greater than the weight of their evil deeds. However, for those who have heard about Jesus and His provision for sins, facing judgment day under their own good works is not a smart option. How could anyone, even with the best of intentions, possibly tilt the scale toward "good" when the heart of a person is desperately wicked, driven by self-preservation instincts, and weighed down daily by selfish ambitions?

In spite of their sophistication and irreverence for God, none of the people in Noah's time who went head-to-head with another element of God's Creation—water—were able to defeat the force of the flood waters or to will themselves away. By succumbing to the floodwater, all those who faced this judgment had to acknowledge that God was indeed LORD over His creation—but it was too late for them.

It is not the amount of knowledge you may acquire about God over your lifetime that will give you access into God's Presence. Everyone will have access to God on the Second Judgment Day, but not everyone will remain in that Presence.[3] The terms of God's free offer are that the only way back to His Presence forever is to confess Jesus as LORD, while we are still alive on earth. At death, we lose forever our free will option to choose God's way versus our own way. Whether you and I make this confession or not, when we come before Him on the Day of Judgment, we will have to bow and declare His Lordship over all of life.

WHY GOD DOES NOT WANT ANY PERSON TO PERISH

Our existence on earth is not an end in itself, but a transition to eternal life. Because He is a righteous God who loves His favorite creation—mankind— God gave the people in Noah's time the greatest possible opportunity to receive His mercy before their eventual death. Noah's ark and his message were well known before the flood. God made His requirement for redemption so obvious, that any person alive in Noah's time—from children to adults—could comprehend God's impending judgment and the provision for escaping it.

Likewise, in our world, the Gospel message and the signs of Jesus' Second Coming are so simple and obvious that anyone willing to submit to God's way can make the connection and the transition. Jesus' Second Coming is to us what the flood was to the people in Noah's time. In John 3:31-36, John the Baptist, the forerunner for Jesus' First Coming proclaimed:

> *The one who comes from heaven is above all. He testifies to what he has seen and heard, but no one accepts his testimony. The man who has accepted it has certified that God is truthful....The Father loves the Son and has placed everything in his hands. Whoever believes in the Son has eternal life, but whoever rejects the Son will not see life, for God's wrath remains on him.*

If you accept the invitation to live life God's way, then you become a born-again human spirit-being, a redeemed soul—freed from the judgement of Adam and Eve. If you reject the invitation, you live on your own terms until you die or until Christ returns—whichever one comes first for you.

What if you die before
the Second Coming?

When I failed to identify the right radio station, the disc jockey on the telephone was not obligated to give me the tickets just because he had called my number. In like manner, when a person rejects God's way, he or she has no reason to expect to be in God's Presence at death. If you die before Jesus' return and you've confessed Him as your LORD before your death, Scriptures teach that your soul will automatically go and dwell in God's Presence.[4] Only in God's Presence can the soul of the righteous find complete solace from its temporary separation from the body.

If Adam and Eve could not dwell in God's Presence after the fall, neither can anyone who rejects God's provision in this lifetime dwell in His Presence in the afterlife. If you reject the Good News Message, your soul will become a wandering soul, dislodged from its natural body, until hell becomes a physical reality. Hell, as a physical destination for Satan and all those who chose to live without God, will not be in session until after the Second Judgment Day. This is why Satan and his companions are wandering spirits with no current permanent address.

Hell, as we have come to know it, is a place of eternal fire and brimstone, reserved for the devil and his followers—both fallen angels and human beings. Until hell becomes an actual physical reality, all the departed souls who die in their sins, naked and uncovered by the blood of the Lamb of God, remain wandering beings like the fallen angels—unable to die, unable to dwell in God's Presence, and consumed by lack because the body is no longer able to respond to its needs. This disoriented abyss—a terrible state of being—is generally referred to as Hades in the Greek and as Sheol in the Hebrew Old Testament. Jesus confirmed this view in the story of Lazarus and the rich man in Luke 16:22-26 (AMP):

> *And it occurred that the man [reduced to] begging died and was carried by the angels to Abraham's bosom. The rich man also died and was buried. And in Hades (the realm of the dead), being in torment, he lifted up his eyes and saw Abraham far away, and Lazarus in his bosom. And he cried out and said, Father Abraham, have pity and mercy on me and send Lazarus to dip the tip of his finger in water and cool my tongue, for I am in anguish in this flame. But Abraham said, Child, remember that you in your lifetime fully received [what is due you in] comforts and delights, and Lazarus in like manner the discomforts and distresses; but now he is comforted here and you are in anguish. And*

> *besides all this, between us and you a great chasm has been*
> *fixed, in order that those who want to pass from this [place]*
> *to you may not be able, and no one may pass from there to*
> *us.*

The fact that a human being who was created in the image and likeness of God could end up as a wandering soul—permanently removed from the possibility of fellowship with God—is bad enough, but burning eternally in a literal hell after the Second Judgment is worse. But this does not have to be the story of your life or of those in your sphere of influence.

Scriptures teach that when Jesus returns, all those whose souls currently dwell in the Presence of God will return with Him and be reunited with their renewed bodies. They will all become like Adam and Eve before the fall. What if a person was cremated at death—how can their body be restored? Remember that in the mystery of the afterlife, we are dealing with a God who spoke the universe into existence and who came down to form mankind from the dirt of the earth. At His Second Coming, this same God will reassemble every human body of those whose souls dwell in His Presence with just one trumpet blast, even from a tiny speck of dirt buried in the deepest ocean.

What if you are still alive at the Second Coming?

If Jesus returns before you physically die, and you've already confessed Him as your LORD, then, just like Enoch, your physical body will be redeemed from the judgment of Adam and Eve. You will rise up to meet your Creator with a spirit, soul, and body that will never again be out of fellowship with God, out of sync with God's purpose, or subject to electromagnetic or gravitational forces.[5]

What if you are left behind?

In order to be redeemed to dwell in God's Presence, those left behind will have to fight against unbearable persecutions relying on their own strength to believe the truth about Jesus and to confess Him as LORD before their death[6] or before the Second Judgment Day (whichever comes first for them). Why anyone would want to take a chance with eternal life instead of accepting the divine free ticket to eternity with God is a mystery, especially when we live a breath away from the commencement of our individual destiny in eternity.

HOW DO WE KNOW FOR SURE?

You may ask—how can all this be? If this were the first time this phenomenon had occurred in the annals of humanity, it would indeed be hard to believe. However, because what will happen has happened before, we are able not only to understand these truths but also to believe them. For instance, we know that in just a twinkling of an eye, Enoch and Elijah were transformed from mortality into immortality.

As both the Son of God and the Son of Man, Jesus lived in a body that was not subject to electromagnetic or gravitational forces, yet He willingly subjected Himself to those powers. Remember the story about Jesus walking on water and challenging Peter to do the same? What about the time the Jews in Jesus' home town were upset at His teachings and drove Him to a cliff to kill Him? The people who tried to push Him over the cliff watched Him walk right by them, and they were unable to physically touch Him.[7]   What about the day of transfiguration, when heaven opened and three of His trembling disciples watched as He conversed with Moses and Elijah? Jesus was crucified because that was to be His lot in this life as God's permanent sacrifice, and He willingly accepted the call of the cross so that no human being would have to perish.

When Jesus rose from the dead on Easter morning, He had the same body, with the physical marks of the cross, yet He was able to enter buildings through the walls and talk at length with two of His disciples on the road to Emmaus. And those two disciples did not recognize Him until He vanished instantaneously. He appeared before His disciples in a closed room without using the door and challenged doubting Thomas to check out His nail pierced hands and feet. He showed up at the Sea of Tiberias where Peter and his companions had been having difficulty fishing, and He made a fire, baked bread, and cooked fish for them for breakfast.

While Jesus was physically seen by hundreds of people in Jerusalem after His resurrection, the tomb where His dead body had been placed remained empty except for the clothes that He had been wrapped in at His burial. Jesus ascended to heaven with the same physical body unrestricted by electromagnetic and gravitational forces, while His disciples looked on in sheer wonder. Acts 1:10-11 reads:

> *They stood there, staring into the empty sky. Suddenly two men appeared—in white robes! They said, "You Galileans!—why do you just stand here looking up at an empty sky? This very Jesus who was taken up from among you to heaven will come as certainly—and mysteriously— as he left.*

Ever since the day of Christ's ascension, all of creation has been eagerly awaiting the day when human beings will again have physical bodies free from gravitational and electromagnetic forces, like Adam and Eve and the sons of God—enabled not by rocket-propelled devices but by the very Spirit that mysteriously raised Jesus from the dead. Depending on how you wager, the mystery of the afterlife will soon show you as a winner or a loser—and there is no consolation prize.

Notes:

1. Revelation 20:13-15.
2. Ecclesiastes 12:13-14 (AMP).
3. 2 Corinthians 5:10.
4. 2 Corinthians 5:6-9.
5. Luke 16:19-31; Revelation 20:7-15.
6. Matthew 24:36-51; 1 Corinthians 15:50-58; 1 Thessalonians 4:14-18; Philippians 3:20-21; 1 John 3:2-3.
7. Revelation 6:7-11; 7:9-17.

Chapter 9

MAKING A NOAH-TYPE DIFFERENCE

In their sophisticated culture, the people in Noah's time either missed or deliberately ignored every sign sending them to their doom. The same sophisticated culture built by the knowledge of good and evil also provides the reason why many in our generation have written off the pursuit of God's purpose and refused to pay any attention to the signs of our own end times. According to Stanley Hauerwas, "Christians in modernity thought their task was to make the Gospel intelligible to the world rather than to help the world understand why it could not be intelligible without the Gospel."

Although almost all of the people in Noah's time took God for granted and thought Him irrelevant, Noah and His family took God seriously. Noah spent one hundred and twenty years obediently building an ark, and dutifully sharing God's good news and bad news to his generation. The bad news message that Noah preached was that the earth was scheduled to be destroyed. The good news message was that none of the people had to die—if they chose to take God's provision for deliverance seriously.

However, one of the most striking attributes of the people in Noah's time was their complacency. The people perished not for lack of knowledge, visible landmarks, or signs of their impending doom, they perished because they abandoned God's purpose for their lives. They refused to take God seriously.

Despite the cynical response from the people of his day, Noah lived righteously, and wholeheartedly pursued God's purpose. The result speaks for itself— Noah and his wife became the parents of modern mankind, and all those who failed to take God seriously became extinct from the annals of humanity. One life can make an enormous difference in the pursuit of God's purpose. It is because of Noah's faithfulness that you and I and over six billion others are alive today. In like manner, there is no reason why you should live this life on earth without the assurance that your eternal life is secured. Once your eternal life status is secured by your belief and confession that Jesus is LORD, then, love God with all your heart and all your intellect, love and serve your fellow human beings, and share with others how to obtain a free ticket to eternity with God.

HOW THEN SHOULD WE LIVE TODAY?

How then should we live today in order to avoid being like the people in Noah's day? Do we try to stop human cloning by stopping any scientific research leading to it? Noah never forced people to follow God's purpose, nor did he campaign to destroy the sons of God (Nephilim) who continued Lamech's immoral strategy for procreation. Whether we like it or not, human cloning is going to be part of our existence in the end times, just as other forms of wickedness will increase. Mankind has become so depraved that some scientist somewhere in the world may have already created a human clone or may be about to do so.

Jesus said that the same things that occurred before the flood would reoccur during our end-time world. King Solomon, in his human wisdom, wrote:

What was will be again, what happened will happen again. There's nothing new on this earth. Year after year it's the same old thing. Does someone call out, "Hey, this is new"? Don't get excited—it's the same old story. Nobody remembers what happened yesterday. And the things that will happen tomorrow? Nobody'll remember them either. Don't count on being remembered.[1]

While Solomon was correct in his observation, we do not have to allow his comments to become prophetic. We can become the generation that remembers what happened in the past and promote enough awareness of God's purpose among our contemporaries so that we are not complacent about human cloning and other global societal ills. Our time on earth is not a time to be apathetic and to sit back and do nothing about making a Godly difference. Perhaps you are alive for such a time as this in order to make a righteous difference in your sphere of influence.

This does not mean that we should allow fear to drive our response and cause physical harm to scientists or seek to shut down biomedical laboratories that engage in stem cell research. We cannot use legislation to take away the funding for biomedical research for the sake of stopping human cloning. Let's not forget that there are far more benefits to humanity that result from biomedical research. We must stay engaged with those in the front lines of stem cell research and provide spiritual and ethical guidance before—and after—half-human, half-something else creatures come to life in scientific laboratories.

The greatest challenge in dealing with human cloning will come when we begin to see an assortment of cloned humans and other creatures—from designer pets to designer babies to obscene hybrids. The process of human cloning has the potential to result in more loss of life than any catastrophic event modern mankind has ever experienced, including the legalization of abortion.

Just as human cloning and its results affected everyone in Noah's time, human cloning in our day is a global issue, and no one country can adequately curtail its practice or abuse worldwide. Yet, we are all responsible for the results. Where possible we ought to seek ways to legally regulate its proliferation. It's okay to watch a story about "Little Mermaid" at a movie theatre, but when your neighbor next door actually clones one, how do you relate to it/he/she?

Balancing our personal values with that of a crazed world will no doubt stretch our belief system. However, we cannot treat human clones who survive to birth and beyond as any less than ourselves. If human cloning leads to our end time, it will be because Christians failed to take Jesus' command seriously. Jesus described our current world perfectly in Matthew 24:7-14 (MSG):

> *Nation will fight nation and ruler fight ruler, over and over. Famines and earthquakes will occur in various places. This is nothing compared to what is coming. They are going to throw you to the wolves and kill you, everyone hating you because you carry my name. And then, going from bad to worse, it will be dog-eat-dog, everyone at each other's throat, everyone hating each other. In the confusion, lying preachers will come forward and deceive a lot of people. For many others, the overwhelming spread of evil will do them in—nothing left of their love but a mound of ashes. Staying with it—that's what God requires. Stay with it to the end. You won't be sorry, and you'll be saved. All during this time, the good news—the Message of the kingdom—will be preached all over the world, a witness staked out in every country. And then the end will come.*

God's purpose for our time is that Jesus returns because Christians did their jobs by ensuring that every person alive knows how to obtain their ticket to eternal life. While it is true that knowing about why a church exists in your neighborhood or knowing about why we have Christmas holidays is a witness that a person has heard the good news, God's desire is that everybody get the opportunity to personally hear the good news message delivered to them by those in their sphere of influence.

Unfortunately, God is far less interested in our church-based revivals that will fill our church pews with disobedient and signs- and wonders-seeking "saints" as He is interested in ensuring that no human being in any nation on earth loses out on the chance to spend eternity with Him. Leslie Newbigin put it well: "The major role of the church in relation to the great issues of justice and peace will not be in its formal announcements but in continually nourishing and sustaining men and women who will act responsibly as believers in the course of their secular duties as citizens."

When human cloning becomes a cosmetic status symbol, our world will have become so depraved

that a description of Noah's world will fit ours
perfectly:

> *GOD saw that human evil was out of control. People*
> *thought evil, imagined evil—evil, evil, evil from morning to*
> *night. GOD was sorry that he had made the human race in*
> *the first place; it broke his heart. GOD said, "I'll get rid of*
> *my ruined creation, make a clean sweep: people, animals,*
> *snakes and bugs, birds—the works. I'm sorry I made them."*
> *But Noah was different. GOD liked what he saw in Noah."*[2]

My prayer is that your name and mine will be
substituted in that last sentence, instead of Noah's in
our end time. May it be written in this generation
that:

_____ (your name) was different.
GOD liked what he saw in _____
(your name).

Ultimately, human cloning will make humanity
as depraved as it was in the time of Noah—and God
will finally declare again, "I'm not going to breathe
life into men and women endlessly."[3] Instead of
another flood, Jesus will return to take those who
believe in Him to heaven. In addition, the Holy Spirit,

who from the time of the fall had restrained the scope of Satan's operations on earth, will also return to heaven.[4] As a result, the level of wickedness during this period will surpass anything humanity has ever known or experienced. The monstrosity of evil that will be unleashed on the earth and upon all remaining humans by an unrestrained devil may never be able to be captured in human words.

Ironically, while modern humankind seeks to make space travel another frontier in human accomplishments (for those who can afford it), God is preparing to give all those who have accepted His free salvation ticket a glorious ride into eternity. Once again, Spirit-Human Beings will have the permanent abilities of God's sons and daughters to be everywhere at the same time, making a mockery of mankind's noble but uncertain pursuit to visit planets so far away and return to the earth in one piece. Remember Lamech and Enoch!

Eventually, this world we know will be destroyed by fire—perhaps sparked by a fallen asteroid or meteorite or a collision with another planet—all of which are proven scientific possibilities and part of the divine master plan.

Finally, if all of this has dampened your spirits, cheer up—God is still in control of His world. God has promised to create a new heaven and a new earth for His beloved and redeemed Human Species. Enjoy life to the fullest in pursuit of God's purpose because, "… he's already made it plain how to live, what to do, what GOD is looking for in men and women. It's quite simple: Do what is fair and just to your neighbor, be compassionate and loyal in your love, And don't take yourself too seriously—take God seriously."[5]

Notes:

1.   Ecclesiastes 1:9-11 (MSG)
2.   Genesis 6:5-8 (MSG).
3.   Genesis 6:3 (MSG).
4.   2 Thessalonians 2:5-12.
5.   Micah 6:8 (MSG).

We would like to thank you for reading this book. Please let us know if you have any suggestions or strategies for dealing with the aftermath of human cloning in our time.

We welcome all religious, ethical, societal, scientific, and medical views.

Visit us at www.Godpurpose.com or write to:

**Sonika Publishing
Human Cloning Issues
P.O. Box 7114
Fremont, CA 94537-7114**

WHEN GOD'S PURPOSE BECOMES...

Come join us as we look back through the years at the history of human interaction with the God of purpose, and discover how the past affects our present day reality. *When God's Purpose Becomes ...* is a series of books that attempts to review God's relationship with mankind over time from God's perspective. These books go beyond theology and dogma to help us deal with the issues of everyday life by learning from the experiences of those who once lived on earth. We will see how our human ancestors functioned both inside and outside God's purpose for their lives, so that we can see our own life experiences reflected in the mirror of their lives. In reading these books, you too will discover why God made you to be special and unique, and why you are living during such a time as this.

Author Biography

Matthew OMAYE Ajiake is an evangelist, author, speaker, recording artist, songwriter-producer, and entrepreneur. He is the President of Global Christian Ambassadors, Inc., an international organization providing global opportunities and platforms for everyday Christians to make a difference in the areas of community development, outreaches, crusades, technology transfers, education, and entertainment.

Matthew is also the CEO of The Sonika Group Corporation, a management, Information Technology, marketing, and organizational development consulting firm. As a global strategist and an organizational and cultural change consultant, Matthew and his team assist individuals and organizations in defining their purpose and in incubating and developing innovative ideas and whole systems that lead to products and services for the global marketplace. Matthew is the former President and CEO of eGlobalRadio and GlobalSportsNow Networks. As the former Corporate Vice President of a multi-billion dollar Silicon Valley Utility, Matthew was responsible for overseeing several of the administrative functions of the organization.

After receiving his biblical training from Simpson College and graduating with a B.A., Matthew earned an M.B.A. from Golden Gate University in San Francisco. Matthew and his wife, Tammy, live in Fremont, California and have five children, Olivia, Jason, Austin, Josiah, and Grace.